WHO GOES NEXT?
True Stories of Exciting Escapes

Of all creatures, man is the most difficult to keep caged. There is no textbook on escape, yet every prison, no matter how "escape proof" it is claimed to be, has lost some of its unwilling guests. Here are twelve true tales of men whose ingenuity and determination would not permit them to languish in confinement. Some were famous, some not; some imprisoned justly, some unjustly, but all had that extra measure of human dignity that would not accept chains.

WHO GOES NEXT?
True Stories of Exciting Escapes

By Robert Edmond Alter
Illustrated by Albert Orbaan

"Hope and the love of liberty never become extinct in the heart of man."
HENRI MASERES DE LATUDE

© 1966 by Robert Edmond Alter
All Rights Reserved

CONTENTS

Prologue 9
1 "No Mortal Thing Can Deter Me" 12
2 Pompadour's Prisoners 29
3 Travail for a Tory 43
4 Like a Thief in the Night 56
5 The Unknown Fact 71
6 The Brink of Eternity 87
7 One Way Out 104
8 The Man from Devil's Island 122
9 To Hang It on a Limb 141
10 The Whim of Chance 162
11 The Fourth Man 174
Index 187

"Since man invented prisons and slavery, the prisoners and the slaves have always attempted to escape, regardless of the price of failure. The battle has gone on for thousands of years. It will go on for thousands of years to come."

ROBERT E. BURNS

WHO GOES NEXT?
True Stories of Exciting Escapes

PROLOGUE

Ever since our first Paleolithic ancestor found himself trapped inside a cave by one of his many savage enemies, the compulsion to escape has been inherent in man.

Next to the love of life the love of liberty is an atavistic motivation with more force than any other impulse in man's libido. Place a man in a cage or in chains, in a hole in the ground or in the cab of a crushed car, and his first instinctive thought will invariably be: *How can I get out?*

To escape prison, or any form of bondage, men have scaled the absolute heights of human courage, fortitude and ingenuity. Their instinct for self-preservation as free men has been so demanding that they would balk at nothing to obtain their ultimate goal. To cite a rather grisly example, here is a sketch of what a man named Schaarschmidt suffered to gain his freedom.

The window of Schaarschmidt's cell was guarded by two oak-beam cross-pieces. The inner barrier was seven by seven inches, the outer nine by nine inches. Being fed only on black bread and water, Schaarschmidt had nothing he could use as a tool — except his teeth. He resolved to gnaw his way to freedom!

In three months the determined man had chewed through the inner wooden bars — carefully filling in the signs of his work each night with a putty made of the bread and water — and in four more months he chewed through the outer bars, and escaped. It is said that his teeth were worn to mere bloody stumps, and his jaw muscles so developed from this remarkable feat of mastication that he looked like an ape.

But every escape — no matter how clever in design — is subject to the element of chance. There is always something unforeseen, something unguessed, something unknown. Sometimes it works in favor of the escaper; more often it throws all his plans awry. The following is a good example of pure chance.

A nobleman had been caught up in the French Revolution and condemned to the guillotine. His hands bound behind his back, he was standing at the foot of the guillotine waiting his turn to be beheaded. Something went wrong with the crank just as it was his turn to mount the fatal steps, and the executioner called for a carpenter.

The crowd pressed in to watch the carpenter work on the guillotine. The nobleman leaned against the people with an air of resignation. Some of them unconsciously shifted aside, and he stepped back again. More of them automatically moved out of his way and he slowly drifted through them until he found himself standing alone at the crowd's back. He strolled around a corner and bumped into a man.

"Citizen," he said, "observe the absurd thing that has happened to me. Some rowdy friends of mine have tied my hands as a joke and have left me in this fix."

The unsuspecting citizen laughed and promptly set him free!

But whether it is a spur-of-the-moment evasion, like the nobleman's, or a seven-month ordeal, such as Schaarschmidt experienced, most exciting of all adventure stories is that of the escaping prisoner; the life-or-death chance taken by a lone fugitive against tremendous odds. This book is a compilation of some of the most amazing escapes ever recorded in history.

In a few instances the known facts regarding the exact details of certain phases of particular escapes are vague, and I have had to resort somewhat to literary invention to bridge the gaps.

The stories are set in three periods: the 18th, 19th and 20th centuries. They are not, however, placed in exact chronological order. It is the purpose of this book to create a pattern of human endeavor — not to establish a strict adherence to dates, which has no bearing on the eternal spirit of Escape.

CHAPTER 1

"No Mortal Thing Can Deter Me"

IN 1743 Baron Friedrich von der Trenck, a seventeen-year-old subaltern in Frederick the Great's royal bodyguard, was conducted to Colonel Jaschinsky's quarters and informed that he was to be imprisoned in the fortress of Glatz in Silesia.

Young Trenck was staggered. He had committed no crime, was not guilty of any military misconduct.

"But for what reason, sir?" he demanded.

"Whatever the reason," the colonel snapped, "it is not my business. Guards! Remove the prisoner."

"But I have not been accused or tried or judged!" Trenck cried.

"The King has already taken care of all that," the colonel said. "You are to be stripped of your rank and conducted to Glatz immediately." His voice held the heavy note of finality.

There was no accusation, no court of inquiry, not even a sentence. In a state of total bewilderment, young Trenck was cashiered from the Prussian army and placed in prison. It was all done by the King's command.

Frederick the Great was an unbalanced egomaniac, and he had taken an unreasoning dislike to the young baron simply because his sister had been charmed by Trenck's personality. He had Trenck incarcerated on a trumped-up charge of treason that was absolutely absurd. But the King's word was law, and Trenck could make no appeal for justice.

Trenck therefore resolved to win his freedom by his own wits.

"I am innocent," he told the governor of Glatz. "I have never been tried and should not be in prison. I shall do everything in my power to regain my liberty. I shall persist in trying to escape until I either succeed or lose my life in the attempt."

He meant what he said. In the next three years Baron Trenck attempted five escapes. In one dramatic attempt he procured a penknife, notched the blade and sawed through eight iron bars on his cell window. Then he sliced his leather portmanteau into thongs, sewed them end to end, added the sheets from his bed and climbed down the face of the citadel's tower — ninety feet — by way of this chancy rope.

It was raining, the night was dark, and everything seemed ideal for his purpose — except that the moat was knee-deep in gluey mud. Trenck fought the morass for hours but was not able to extricate himself. Realizing his position was hopeless, he gave up at dawn and shouted for the astonished sentry, calling:

"Go inform the governor that Trenck is stuck fast in the moat!"

Another hair-raising attempt was made when three officers came to Trenck's cell one day to examine every corner of his room. A major started a tirade against Trenck, claiming that the young baron had committed "a second crime" by endeavoring to escape.

There was no plan in Trenck's mind when he suddenly went into action. He simply saw his chance and took it.

He snatched the major's sword from its scabbard, sprang through the open door, tumbled the sentry outside the cell down the staircase, and started running through the corridors. He ran right into a large group of soldiers who had come to relieve the guard.

Trenck caught them by surprise and hacked his way through, wounding four of them. Darting through an archway he gained the ramparts and, without hesitation, sword in hand, leaped over the parapet and dropped into the yard below without hurting himself.

None of the guards had the courage to leap after him, and for a vivid moment it looked as though Trenck would reach the palisade and make good his escape.

He encountered a sentry in a narrow passage and parried the man's bayonet and wounded him in the face. Instantly a second sentry ran from the outworks to grab him from behind and Trenck made a desperate spring at the palisade.

His foot caught. A bayonet sliced his lip. He was surrounded and beaten with musket butts and dragged back to prison, struggling and defending himself like a madman.

Trenck's fifth attempt at freedom occurred in 1746 when he made friends with a Lieutenant Schell of the guards. Schell himself was in bad with the governor, and when a friend warned him that he was going to be relieved from duty and placed under arrest, Schell snatched up a saber and hurried to Trenck's cell.

"I'm in trouble!" he whispered. "Let's make a bolt for it together. But one thing — don't let them take me alive."

They walked out of the cell and Schell said to the sentry:

"I'm taking the prisoner to the anteroom. Stand where you are."

Once in the anteroom, they passed out by another door and gained the outer ramparts. They walked right into the two officers who were coming to arrest Schell!

Schell sprang to the parapet and went over the wall, which was not very high at that spot, and Trenck jumped after him. Trenck landed unhurt but Schell had twisted his ankle. They still had the palisade to leap and Schell couldn't walk. He drew his saber and handed it to Trenck.

"Kill me and run for it!"

Trenck refused to comply. Instead, he picked up Schell and dropped him over the palisade, jumped over himself, and then, carrying his crippled friend on his back, ran into the twilight fog. The alarm guns were fired before they had gone a hundred yards.

"It's hopeless," Schell said despairingly. "We'll never make it like this. You're simply laboring in vain."

Trenck refused to listen. "Death or freedom," he gasped. "I've made up my mind to that."

The alarm had now sounded in the surrounding villages and all the garrison troops, as well as hundreds of peasants, came out to help in forming the encircling ring. Trenck struggled down to the River Neiss and started wading.

It was December and there was ice in the river. Trenck waded through the freezing water until the bottom dropped beneath his feet. Then he had Schell cling to his neck and he started to swim. He found bottom again within six yards and they reached the other bank. Day found them on the road to Silesia. They had traveled about twenty miles, having stolen first a rowboat and then two horses, and now they were at the frontier and safety.

At the town of Braunau, Trenck sent the saber and the two horses back to the governor of Glatz with a mocking letter. Only the day before, the governor had publicly stated that it was quite impossible for Baron Trenck to escape.

Frederick the Great was not a forgiving man. For eight years — while Trenck roamed Europe as a soldier of fortune — the Prussian king plotted his vengeance. His opportunity came in 1754.

Trenck's mother had died in Danzig and he went there to settle her estate. Danzig was a free town at that time, but Trenck had hardly entered the city gate when Frederick's agents pounced on him.

He was taken to the Star Fort at Magdeburg and placed in a cell that Frederick had already prepared for him. It was in a casemate six feet by ten feet and there were three doors between his cell and the corridor. The walls were seven feet thick and there were iron bars within and without his single window. His food allowance was a pound and a half of bread per day and a jug of water.

"You will never escape this prison, Baron," the governor said.

"No mortal thing can deter me from attempting to obtain my freedom," Trenck answered.

The three doors were kept perpetually locked except for one day a week, when the governor came to inspect Trenck and his cell. Trenck received his pittance of bread and water through an aperture in the wall. This arrangement gave him an excellent opportunity to work out a plan of escape without being observed.

His cell contained a stool which was secured to the floor by iron strips eighteen inches long. Laboring night and day he was able to work loose one of these strap-irons. Now he had a tool.

He went to work on the wall. The first layer was

"No Mortal Thing Can Deter Me" 19

brick, and behind that were large hewn stones. It was tedious labor and it necessitated intricate planning. Each brick and stone had to be numbered so that it could be set back in place before the governor made his weekly visit. This included the outer mortar.

The wall had been whitewashed, and in order to fill in the chinks he flaked off and pounded up some of the whitewash, wetted it, made a brush of his own hair and applied this plaster to the chinks to make the wall appear uniform. Then he sat with his naked back against the place and dried it with his body heat.

It was impossible to replace all of the mortar and brick- and stone-chips, so he scattered the residue on the floor and ground it to dust underfoot. Placing this dust in the aperture of his window, he made a sort of broom by tying splinters of his bedstead together with the unraveled yarn of his stocking and affixed tufts of his hair to one end of it. Then he brushed the dust as far as he could through the aperture and let the night wind blow it away.

The labor of penetrating through the seven-foot wall was incredible. The fort was an ancient pile, and much of the mortar had petrified, which often forced Trenck to reduce a whole stone to dust. It took him six long months to reach the outer facing of brick. Freedom was only inches away.

Then disaster struck.

Trenck had just replaced all the stones in his tunnel and camouflaged the entrance when a group of officers walked in.

"Gather up your bedding, Baron," one of them said.

"We are taking you to a new cell."

Six torturous months of unremitting labor for nothing!

Trenck's new dungeon was built in the ditch of the Star Fort. The stone walls were six feet thick and there were four double doors to the corridor. One end of a chain was fixed to his ankle, the other to a ring built in the wall. A huge iron ring was then riveted around his body, to which hung a chain clamped to an iron bar which had a handcuff at each end.

Escape seemed impossible, yet Trenck still refused to submit to his unjust fate. In his own words: "I glowed with the desire of convincing the world that I was capable of suffering what man had never suffered before — perhaps of at last emerging from this load of wretchedness and triumphing over my enemies."

Gritting his teeth with pain he forced his hands through the cuffs, the blood spurting from under his fingernails. Setting his back to the wall and making a Herculean effort he was able to bend open the hook that connected the chain to the ring around his body. Again with incredible strength, he doubled the ankle-chain links and wrenched and strained until one link flew off.

The double doors were of oak, two inches thick. Trenck had concealed his tool in his clothes and he now went to work gouging out the wood around the lock-plate. He knew he had only twenty-four hours before the guards returned, and he worked frenziedly in the pitch dark, his fingers clotted with his own blood.

One door opened ... then another ... daylight appeared ... the third door was open and he started on the last . . . time was running out . . . something went *snap*, and the broken tool dropped to the ground!

He was placed in chains again and his spirit fell to a low ebb.

The conditions in his cell were impossible. He was continually wet to the skin with icy water that dripped on him from the vaulted roof. He fell sick and was incapacitated for months. No doctor came to see him; he was given no medicine; he was nearly skin and bones when his unconquerable fortitude began to revive.

He made friends with a sentry named Gelfhardt, and the man was kind enough to smuggle a small file into the cell. Trenck filed his way out of the chains and contrived a way to trick the guards when they made their daily inspection. He filled the fracture in each cut link with bread rubbed over the rusty iron. The camouflage was perfect. Now he had the freedom of his cell.

The floor was wide oak planking held together by huge nails a foot long and half an inch thick. Trenck prised one of them out, sharpened the end with his file and made a chisel. Then he cut out one of the planks and went to work digging a tunnel under the wall of his cell.

The fort was built on white sand, which made for easy digging, but the problem was — what to do with the sand? He could always replace the plank and fill the cut with dirt-rubbed bread, to pass inspection, but there was no way to conceal the sand.

There was a small grilled aperture leading to the ditch, and though it was too small to emit a man, Gelfhardt was able to pass some yards of cloth through it. Trenck cut them into long narrow bags, filled them with earth and sand, filed an opening in the grill and stuffed the bags out to Gelfhardt, who scattered the contents in the ditch and passed the bags back.

Trenck's hole was four feet deep and just wide enough for him to kneel and stoop in. He had to lie down to dig, then get up and stoop over like a dog to throw out the sand between his legs, and the narrow space in which all these evolutions had to be performed made the labor incredible. And after this backbreaking daily toil everything had to be replaced and his chains put on again.

To add to the difficulties, Gelfhardt mounted guard only once a fortnight and so the work progressed very slowly. Then winter came and Trenck suffered greatly without heat. Moreover, the governor suspected that Trenck might possibly be contemplating another break for freedom and he ordered that a monstrous iron collar be clapped around the baron's neck and fastened to his ankle chains. Trenck fell sick again.

Racked with fever, trembling with cold, suffering fearful headaches, his swollen neck inflamed by the iron collar, Trenck nearly died. He laid in a comatose state for over two months before he began a long, painful recovery.

His spirit revived with his body; but Gelfhardt brought him bad news. The sentries had been doubled and the ditch was now under constant patrol.

"You will have to change the direction of your tunnel and dig toward the entrance of the gallery in the main rampart," he said.

"How far is this gallery?"

"Thirty-seven feet."

"No Mortal Thing Can Deter Me" 23

Trenck had now been in Magdeburg for nearly three years and the news that he would have to dig thirty-seven feet through dirt and sand and foundation stones, with nothing but his bare hands and a makeshift chisel, was vastly disheartening.

But Trenck's motto was Death or Freedom. He started to dig.

His greatest fear now was that the noise of his digging would be heard by the numerous sentries, so he relied more on his bare hands than on his chisel. His progress was appallingly slow, and the worst of it was that Gelfhardt could only rarely find an opportunity to scatter the dirt and sand for him.

Each day Trenck had to scoop up all the sand he had emptied out of the tunnel, sack it and store the bags back in the hole. This consumed a great deal of time and energy, as did the careful replacing of the floor planks and the resuming of his chains. The fatiguing labor of one night's work was so severe that he would be forced to rest the following three days.

In this manner it took him six months to go ten feet. Then he encountered the foundation of the rampart. He could not remove the stones because he could not dispose of them, so he had to dig a U-shaped dip to pass under them. The sand was damp and there was water at this new level.

The work dragged like a wounded turtle into months and on into years, until one day Trenck found himself only three feet from his objective. Then fate stepped in on him again.

A sentry put his ear to the ground and heard Trenck filling up his hole with the sandbags. He called the officer of the guard and they entered the cell only a few minutes after Trenck had replaced the last stone. The major in charge was a rather stupid fellow and he found nothing wrong.

"Idiot!" he said to the sentry. "It was a mole you heard, not Trenck. How could it possibly be he at work underground at such a distance from his dungeon!"

Trenck was convinced that his time was now very short, and as soon as the soldiers left he rushed to his tunnel to make his last effort at escape. But the sentry who had heard him before was still on duty and once again he heard Trenck burrowing. He called for the guard and the major and all of them went into the gallery and listened.

The first Trenck knew of it was when he looked back along the tunnel and saw a light. He was thunderstruck. The game was obviously up and the guards were patiently awaiting for him to emerge from his hole. Discouraged, Trenck crawled back over the sand he had thrown behind him and went out to face them.

The tunnel was filled up, the masonry replaced, and Trenck was chained in new fetters. The guards made only one mistake: they forgot to search his clothes. Trenck still had his file.

He was so exhausted from his last undertaking that he was little better than a skeleton. Again he was attacked by a violent fever and succumbed to illness. Six long months elapsed before he recovered enough strength to make a new bid for freedom.

The obvious course was to mine through his old

tunnel; but first he had to rid himself of some of the sand in the hole. He filed through his chains, opened the tunnel and started pitching the sand onto the floor of his cell. That done, he closed the hole and began digging a second hole — this one under the door.

He made as much noise as he could so that the sentries would be bound to hear him and, as he had expected, they came into his cell and found him hard at work.

They hauled *all* his sand away in wheelbarrows, boarded up the new hole and replaced his fetters. They thought he was crazy to dig out under the door where there was a triple guard to pass, and they were so busy laughing at his foolishness that none of them had the sense to notice that three times as much sand was removed as the false hole could possibly contain.

Trenck returned to his daily labor: remove the planks, remove the filled bags, dig, throw out the sand, scoop up every grain and put it in the bags, place the bags back in the hole, replace the planks and climb into his chains . . . over and over and over again, day after month after year; always wet, hungry and enfeebled by exhaustion, with intervals of violent sickness.

Ten feet . . . twenty feet . . . thirty feet. Then a day of horror.

He was mining under the foundations of the rampart and he was just about to wiggle backward with a sandbag when his foot dislodged a stone in the wall above.

The stone dropped with a muffled thump and closed up the passage. Trenck found himself buried alive in a space smaller than a grave pit. He couldn't go ahead, couldn't go back, couldn't turn on either side. The horror of claustrophobia and suffocation swept over him and he almost went mad.

Slowly his scattered wits returned and he began to dig away the damp sand on one side, tossing it into the space ahead of him.

The air soon became so foul he thought he was strangling, and his head began to throb like a drum, and he seemed to be breathing sand. He redoubled his efforts — but presently the space ahead of him became full up and there was nowhere else to put the sand that he scooped out.

Frantic now, he struggled to draw his knees up to his chin and finally managed to turn around. He was facing the fallen stone.

Clawing like a ratter going after a gopher, he was able to dig away the sand under the stone until it sank lower in earth and made an opening at the top through which he could breathe fresher air.

More digging lowered the obstacle until he was able to creep over it and, completely exhausted in mind and body, he crawled back to his cell.

The cave-in gave him a frightful trauma. He could not shake the horror of it from his mind, and for months after he could not bring himself to go near the tunnel. His dreams were haunted by the experience.

Finally his courage took an upswing and he resumed work on his tunnel — but he always took along his sharpened file, to use on himself should such a disaster happen again, knowing that over the stone which had fallen there were several other stones all hanging loosely, and under these stones he had to crawl hundreds of times before he finally reached the gallery.

His work was completed late in 1763. He had been a prisoner in Magdeburg's Star Fort for over nine years. All he had to do was break through the gallery floor and hop over the rampart.

He didn't do it. Instead, he called for the officer of the guard.

What Trenck did at this point is almost inconceivable. Some historians suggest that he had suffered too much for too long, that his mind had cracked; while others maintain that the wily baron knew exactly what he was doing — risking his ace in the hole on a wild gamble.

Knowing that a prince of the royal house was at that time visiting Magdeburg he threw himself on this sovereign's mercy, saying:

"Tell the prince that I have dug a tunnel and can escape whenever I like, and that I will do so unless the prince promises me his protection."

The officer quickly reported to the governor, who rushed to Trenck's cell and demanded proof of his statement. Trenck showed him the completed tunnel. It was a staggering revelation and the governor promptly had the baron placed in the guardroom while the masons walled up the tunnel and paved his cell with flagstones.

It was a very bad time for Trenck. It looked as

though his gamble had failed and he was about to lose everything. Then, at the last moment, a messenger arrived from Berlin with an order for Trenck's release.

In 1764 Baron Trenck walked out of prison a free man.

Baron Trenck lived to the ripe age of 68 — and might have grown even riper had he not made the mistake of visiting Paris in 1791 during the time of the French Revolution. The new French dictator Maximilien Robespierre had him arrested as an Austrian spy and thrown into prison. The baron was executed by the guillotine in 1794.

CHAPTER 2

Pompadour's Prisoners

ON a bright, clear day in the Paris of 1754 a young prisoner by the name of d'Aligre was conducted to a large gloomy cell high up in the impregnable and escape-proof Bastille.

As the door was locked behind him d'Aligre saw that he was to share the cell with another inmate. A young man was lying on his stomach on the tile floor teaching a pet rat a trick. Other rats hovered nearby as if awaiting their turn.

The young man stood up with a smile and introduced himself to d'Aligre.

"I am Henri Masères de Latude."

D'Aligre had heard of Latude; in fact, all of Paris knew of the man who had been placed in prison simply because he had tried to play a boyish prank on Madame de Pompadour, the King's mistress.

He had been incarcerated in the prison at Vincennes in 1749 at the age of twenty-three. A year later he had made a daring escape by boldly bluffing four sentries in a row. He had then thrown himself on the King's mercy and requested a pardon. Madame Pompadour would have none of it, and Louis XV promptly placed Latude in the Bastille — condemned to a sentence of "forever and a day."

Mme. de Pompadour

D'Aligre was also in the Bastille thanks to the King's mistress, having written a satirical verse about her reputation. This gave the two young prisoners a mutual bond: a hatred of La Pompadour and a burning determination to win their freedom.

"Patience and courage, *mon ami*, and we are saved," Latude said.

He knew it was impossible to attempt to escape the Bastille by the corridors and gates; every physical obstacle imaginable barricaded that path. That left only one alternative: the air.

There was a fireplace in their cell and the chimney rose twenty-five feet to the roof of their tower. It was guarded by a heavy iron grill, the bars of which were set deep in the stone and secured by mortar. This did not discourage Latude.

"We will remove the grill with tools," he told his friend, "climb up the chimney on a ladder and crawl along the parapet to the next tower. Then, by way of a rope, we'll drop the 150 feet into the moat and scale the outer wall."

"Impossible!" d'Aligre cried. "What tools? What ladder? Where is the rope? We have nothing to use for implements!"

It was true; they were not permitted even a table knife. And even if they had tools there was no place in the bare stone cell where they could hide them. The prisoners were always under a close surveillance and their cell was inspected daily.

Latude's plan seemingly called for more than the impossible. It would require enormous courage, ingenuity and strength, and both men were already emaciated from confinement — especially Latude, who had been imprisoned nearly six years.

"We will make them," Latude said grimly. "We will make everything we need, and we will be saved."

First he needed a hiding place for the tools he intended to make. He had an idea about that. Every Sunday they were led down two flights of steps to the chapel, and Latude had noticed that the cell directly beneath theirs was empty. He contrived a plan to enable him an opportunity to inspect this cell.

On the following Sunday when their turnkey led them from the chapel back to their cell, Latude gave d'Aligre a nod and d'Aligre pretended to accidentally drop his toothpick case. It clattered to the bottom of the stairs and the disgruntled turnkey had to go down and get it for him.

Latude instantly darted over to the empty cell, swung open the door and examined the height of the chamber from floor to ceiling. About ten and a half feet. The guard returned and marched the two prisoners up the second flight of stairs. Latude counted the steps between the two landings, estimated the height of one of them and made a quick calculation.

Voila! There was a difference in height between the ceiling of the empty cell below and the floor of their cell of over four feet. The perfect place to hide their implements had been found.

Their first tools were the two iron hooks which supported their table. They gave them a chisel-edge by whetting the ends on the tiled floor. With these tools they grouted out the mortar around some of the floor tiles and found a roomy space between the two cells.

The problem of the iron grill inside the fireplace was awesome. It was set at such an awkward height that they could neither stand nor kneel to work on it with their chisels, but had to crouch and twist their bodies into painful positions. An hour at a time was all they could bear and by then their hands would be raw and bleeding.

To soften the mortar holding the bars they blew mouthfuls of water at it as they worked, but even so there were many nights when they were only able to make an eighth of an inch dent around the adamant bars. It took them six months of incessant labor to remove the grill. Their work was only beginning.

They converted their steel tinderbox into a penknife and with this they made a saw out of their iron candlestick. They sawed their firewood (rough, green sticks provided daily) into eight-inch lengths. This was the beginning of the twenty-foot ladder.

Latude made an auger out of a screwbolt from his bedstead, and they were able to drill the holes for the rungs in the pieces of wood. They made a groove and tongue in the ends of each piece, joined them one into the other, and secured each with two holes and two pegs to prevent swagging. Still and all, it was probably the most rickety ladder ever constructed!

To escape the constant surveillance of the guards they could work only at night, replacing all their tools and ladder-lengths in the hole in the floor just before dawn, and then removing every trace of their nocturnal employment. A single chip of stone or a shaving of wood might betray them.

They also had to deceive the ears of their sentries, who had a nasty habit of listening to the prisoners through small Judas holes set in the walls of the cells. As a precaution against being overheard they invented a dictionary, giving each implement a code name. The saw was called "the monkey"; the iron hooks, "Tubalcain"; the hole, "Polyphemus" (an allusion to Cyclops' cave); the ladder, "Jacob"; and the penknife, "the puppy dog," and so on.

One morning at dawn a turnkey suddenly walked in on them for a surprise inspection. It was nearly their undoing. Quite certain that they had hidden all their escape gear in Polyphemus, they had just barely climbed into bed. Latude stood up to allow the turnkey to search his person. At that moment he happened to glance at the table.

The candlestick saw was lying there in plain sight. They had overlooked it in the dark!

"The monkey is looking for food," he said in a casual voice.

The turnkey undoubtedly thought Latude was making reference to him; but d'Aligre gave a start and shot a glance at the table. Then, in a listless manner, he strolled over and picked up a napkin, wiped his hands and dropped the napkin over the exposed saw.

The turnkey searched d'Aligre, snooped through their beds and spare linen, glanced around at the cell and went away satisfied.

Their completed ladder was so flimsy that they were afraid to subject it to a trial test in the chimney. Too much strain would only serve to weaken it. They decided to wait until the time of the actual escape, contenting themselves meanwhile with testing short sections of it against the walls of their cell.

It was now time to make the rope ladder.

"How on earth can we do it?" d'Aligre fretted. "What can we possibly use for material?"

Smiling, Latude went over to his wardrobe trunk and said, "This trunk holds more than a thousand feet of rope."

"Have you lost your senses?" d'Aligre cried. "I know exactly what your trunk contains — there is not a single inch of rope!"

"In this trunk I have a vast quantity of linen," Latude said. "Fourteen dozen shirts, many napkins, stockings, nightcaps and table cloths. We will unravel them and we will make a rope."

It is an interesting and ironic side glance at the eighteenth century that — although a gentleman could be condemned to a filthy prison for life without a trial — it was unthinkable that any gentleman prisoner would not be allowed a sufficient supply of linen.

Strand by strand they unraveled their linen, and twisted, knotted, spliced it into twine, and then into ropes that would hold a man's weight. On top of that, each rung and mortised joint in their ladder had to be secured with this twine, and before they were done they had woven 1400 feet of it. This included a safety rope. They meant to leave nothing to chance.

Next came the tedious job of making the rungs for the rope ladder. Each wooden rung had to be notched at either end to fit snugly in the splayed rope holes. Latude estimated that 208 rungs would be required; but the green wood, plus their faulty tools, spoiled rung after rung. Before they were finally finished with the chore they had manufactured 600 rungs.

Their preparations were complete. Everything was ready. It had taken them eighteen long months.

They now had the means to reach the top of the tower and to gain the bottom of the moat. From that point they had the choice of two avenues of escape. The first was to climb over the moat parapet to the governor's garden, and from there to descend into the outer ditch of the Porte St. Antoine.

This would be the quickest way, but it had a certain risk. The parapet was heavily patrolled by sentries who made the Grand Rounds and who always carried lanterns.

The second plan made for more labor but was less dangerous. It consisted of digging a tunnel through the moat wall to the outer base of the Porte St. Antoine tower. Latude was not in favor of this latter method because he knew that the moat wall was four and a half feet thick — solid stone and mortar.

"Well," he said, "we will just have to make our final decision when we get there, according to the circumstances."

D'Aligre agreed. There was nothing else they could do.

Wednesday, the night of February 25, 1756. Thick black storm clouds crowded over Paris. It had been raining for days, but now that had stopped and a frost was spreading over the city, and there was ice in the River Seine.

The turnkey brought them their supper and locked them in for the night. They had fashioned a bulky sort of portmanteau out of d'Aligre's leather trunk and they filled it with food they had saved during the last week, with a change of clothes for each of them, and with their tools and the rope ladder.

Working in a fever of excitement they pegged and bound the thirty pieces of their wood ladder together and shoved it up the chimney section by section. The passage was too narrow for the ladder to lean at an angle and there was no way of making it secure at the top. Latude went first.

The rungs projected only three inches beyond the joined uprights and it was nearly impossible to keep his feet from slipping off. He had to hold the ladder with both hands and brace his back against the opposite wall of the chimney.

It was pitch black. The soot began to rain on him. He could barely breathe. The ladder tipped out of balance occasionally because four centuries of rats and decay had honeycombed the walls.

The ladder thumped and buckled against the cheesy walls. The rungs worked loose and skinned his fingers on the soot-crusted stones. His feet slipped off and he slammed into the wall and felt the ladder lurch under him. He clung like a leech, bleeding, suffocating in soot-dust — found his footing and went on up.

A square of sullen sky appeared above him. He climbed for it, gasping with fatigue and emotion. His head came up into clean night air.

Latude climbed to the rim of the chimney and straddled it. For an exhausted moment he stared out at the lights of the city he had not seen in seven years. Then he let down the ball of twine he had carried aloft and d'Aligre tied it to the suitcase.

Latude hauled up the bag and secured the upper end of the ladder to the stack. "Come up!" he whispered down the chimney.

D'Aligre, with the ladder made fast, had a much easier ascent than Latude had experienced. They huddled together on the lip of the chimney and lowered the portmanteau to the Bastille's flat roof.

The sky still threatened a storm but there was no rain, and so the sentries were busy clomping along the frosty Rounds way below them. Latude and d'Aligre made their way across the roof to the next tower, called La Tour du Trésor.

They fastened one end of the rope ladder to the breech of a cannon and lowered the other end gently down the wall until it touched the moat 150 feet below. Then they secured their safety rope and paid it out through a rounded block that Latude had constructed to keep the rope from fraying on the roof tiles.

Latude stepped onto the rope ladder, took the safety rope in his right hand and went over the edge of the roof.

There was four feet of space between the wall and the overhanging cornice, and within thirty feet the wind began to push at the man dangling on the rope ladder. He was swept against the wall, banged brutally, whirled about and lost his footing.

The wind snatched the ladder away from him and he was left swinging on the safety rope. He hung there, kicking at the rope ladder with his feet, trying frantically to bring it back to him.

One hundred feet below and on the opposite side of the moat, the sentry tramped the Rounds with his lantern. Latude watched him go by . . . then his feet tangled in the ladder and he drew it in and caught it in his left hand.

In a few minutes he landed on the cobble curb of the moat and gave three tugs on the safety rope. D'Aligre hauled up the rope, attached the portmanteau to it and lowered it down. D'Aligre started down himself, gaining quite an advantage, because Latude had secured the bottom of the ladder to a dungeon window, which greatly prevented its swinging.

Crouching on the curbing over the black moat, they

ate some of their food to revive their strength. Then they started to explore the first avenue of escape.

There was still no rain and the sentries were making the Grand Rounds with a methodical precision. It would be impossible for the two fugitives to escape over the parapet and into the governor's garden. That left only the second avenue — the hard one.

There was nearly five feet of icy water in the moat, and it was 120 feet wide.

"It is the only possible way," Latude said. "So we will take it."

They lowered themselves into the water and waded across the moat, hauling the bulky portmanteau between them, their heads barely above the surface.

The point Latude had picked to tunnel was at the joint of the outer wall and the gate tower of St. Antoine. They drew their tools from the bag and went to work. They were standing in freezing water to their armpits, and the sentries paced back and forth only forty feet above their heads.

Luckily, they had a grand ally in the whimpering wind that swept up the noise of their digging and blew it away from the ears of the sentries. Also, the centuries of water in the moat had softened and rotted the mortar in the wall and they found the digging here much easier than it had been in the chimney.

D'Aligre gave a warning and Latude glanced up. A patrol major was going along the Rounds with a lantern and its glare cast a halo of light on the spot where the two fugitives were working.

They had no alternative. They ducked their heads under the icy water for a slow count of ten, giving the patrolman time to pass. He returned every fifteen minutes.

Shivering, chipping, ducking, removing one stone at a time, it took them nine hours to break through the wall. They now had a hole, yes, but it was not yet large enough to allow them egress.

Feverishly, they enlarged their tunnel until they could just manage to squeeze and wiggle their emaciated bodies through.

Trembling violently, they stood in the black shadows of the angle formed by the gate tower and the drawbridge leading to the Avenue de St. Antoine. The first faint suggestion of dawn was just starting. A churchbell chimed five times.

Altogether they had spent eleven hours on their escape.

Time was running out. Within the hour the turnkey would enter their cell and find them gone and sound the alarm. Clinging to the dense shadows, they started to run. It was a mistake.

An unseen aqueduct lay waiting for them in the dark. They ran right into it.

Latude pitched headlong into the muddy water and d'Aligre piled helplessly on top of him. The ditch was only six feet wide but it was ten feet deep and clogged with gluey mud. D'Aligre panicked and clutched at Latude. The black water was running swiftly; they floundered, choking, started to go under — d'Aligre wouldn't let go.

Latude gave his comrade a violent blow with his fist. It broke d'Aligre's hold and Latude was able to haul himself out of the mud and onto the stones. Then he felt around for d'Aligre, caught him by the hair and drew him to safety.

Knowing that the hue and cry would shortly be after them, they decided to part company to reduce suspicion. They made arrangements to meet in Belgium.

"Bonne chance, mon ami!" Latude said to his friend.

"I will see you in Belgium, Henri," d'Aligre replied.

Latude made it; d'Aligre did not.

By the time Latude reached Belgium, d'Aligre had been arrested. Latude then slipped into Austria and later into Holland, but he could not find sanctuary anywhere. Prompted by political pressure, the Dutch government handed him over to the French.

Latude made one more successful escape from the Bastille, only to be arrested shortly after. All in all he spent 35 years in prison. However, he became the symbol of hope and determination to all oppressed Frenchmen; he was the *cause célèbre* in the flames of their coming revolution. And, in a sense, he had his revenge. He was present on July 14, 1789, the day when the French masses captured the hated Bastille.

CHAPTER 3

Travail for a Tory

ONE of the prisoners in the teamster's wagon was a very lucky man — at least he thought so at that time. The Continental army had found him guilty of harboring a Tory spy in his home in Clinton, N.Y., and they had ordered him to be shot. Later they had commuted his sentence to imprisonment for the duration of the war.

It was the summer of 1776, and the Revolutionary War had been raging up and down the land for over a year. The prisoner's name was John Byam. He was a mild-mannered farmer with Loyalist sympathies and he had never intended to take an active part in the war. The Tory spy had come to Byam's home and asked for shelter for the night. Not realizing the man was a spy, Byam had taken him in. That had been his big mistake.

The local militia had arrested Byam and the Committee of Safety had turned him over to the Continental army for trial. He was of course innocent of any crime, but the fact remained that he was himself a Tory. He was condemned: first to death, then to imprisonment. He and the other three Tories in the wagon were now being conducted to the Simsbury Mines in Connecticut.

Simsbury had a bad name in that violent year. The

damp, the lack of food, the prevalence of disease made the prison a nightmare. One of the prisoners in the wagon said he would prefer a quick death on the battlefield to the interminable agony of such a prison.

John Byam paid little attention to this kind of talk. He was simply glad to be alive and he thought that was enough for any man. He had yet to learn that a man entombed in a living death was not strictly speaking alive.

The prison itself was called Newgate and it was backed up to a high hill. The prisoners were ordered out of the wagon and herded through a door set in the face of the hill. They were led into a room containing a brazier's furnace, where two grim men were standing with hammers beside an anvil.

"New shackles cost twenty shillings, or you can have old rusty ones for free," the officer of the guard told the prisoners.

Byam had no money. Handcuffs were hammered onto his wrists, joined by a long link chain. Then a pair of linked manacles were fitted to his ankles. When the officer said, "Come this way," Byam found he could hardly manipulate himself in the cumbersome load of chains.

A trapdoor was opened, and the prisoners bumbled down a steep ladder to the guardroom which was twelve feet deep in the mine. Another trapdoor awaited them. It emitted a damp stagnant-water smell and it was very dark.

"Down you go," the officer said.

The prisoners started down an iron ladder. The rungs

were slimy, and their chains clashed and clanged. Then the trapdoor slammed over their heads. There was a very feeble gray light which filtered down from somewhere overhead. Byam had the impression he was descending into an enormous cavern.

It was exactly that: a huge cavern that had been used as a shaft for the mining of copper. Far up in the rocky ceiling was a small circular opening with a grill over it. It was seventy-four feet to fresh air.

There was a little beach of damp sand at the base of the ladder, and there was a large subterranean pool stretching off into the dim distance. About forty men were huddled on the patch of sand, wrapped in scraps of blankets. They had loose straw for mattresses. There were three charcoal braziers which burned twenty-four hours a day. Even so, the cavern was dank and cold.

Byam started to shiver as he looked around. He was appalled by what he saw. It seemed impossible that even a brute beast could live in such impossible conditions.

"The guards take us up to the yard every other day," one of the veteran prisoners told Byam. "But if we make any trouble, they keep us down here and take away our charcoal."

"What can be accomplished by making trouble?" Byam wondered.

The prisoner shrugged. "Sometimes one of us will go mad. Then we all go a little crazy. The guards don't like the noise."

The prisoners took turns tending the braziers. It was vital to their lives that the fires should never go out, and it was a rule that if any man went to sleep while tending fire the other prisoners would throw him in the icy pool. It took a man nearly two weeks to dry out.

John Byam rotted in Simsbury Mine for over a year. In that time history was marching thunderously along in the outside world. Benedict Arnold halted the British invasion on Lake Champlain. Washington lost the battle of Long Island but won the vital battles of Trenton and Princeton. And Arnold and Daniel Morgan beat and captured Burgoyne's entire army at Saratoga.

This latter news was sad tidings for the sorry wretches in the mine. They had hoped Burgoyne's invasion would be a success and that they would be rescued. Their guards laughed at them through the trapdoor and shouted down more bad news to torment them.

"John Stark whipped the Hessians at Bennington! And Benedict Arnold tricked your General St. Leger at Fort Stanwix and made him retreat back to Canada, where all you blasted Tories belong!"

The half-demented Tory prisoners began howling, which created an unholy medley of echoes in the huge cavern. It was a maddening sound and Byam had to cover his ears. He thought about Ft. Stanwix. It was near his home. Then he started thinking about home.

He would never see his home again if he didn't get out of the mine soon, because the appalling conditions of the place would kill him. Some of the prisoners were already dead.

One of them had gone mad and thrown himself in the pool and drowned in his heavy chains. Another had been tossed in the water by his own comrades because he had fallen asleep while tending fire. He had died of pneumonia. Still another had gone berserk because of the continuous drip-drip-dripping of the wet walls and had hammered out his brains against the bare rock.

The dripping water . . . odd he had never thought of it before. The water never stopped dripping off the walls and yet the pool never changed its level. Why was that? There could be only one answer: the cavern had an outlet — somewhere.

Where?

Byam got up and hobbled down the shelving beach in his chains to the edge of the pool. Far off across the dark water he could barely discern two low tunnel-like openings. One of them, he thought, must be the outlet.

Which?

An emotion he had never before known in his mild life sent a shiver through him: excitement! He started wading into the cold water, trying to see across the dark pool.

"Hey! Have you gone mad?" someone called to him. "That's too deep to wade in. You'll drown like Mapes did."

Byam came back to the beach and sat down by one of the braziers to think. The pool was too deep to wade, and he couldn't hope to swim it with forty pounds of iron on his body. So . . .

A raft, he thought. *I'll have to make a raft.*

He knew that some of the fortunate prisoners who had money had purchased pieces of board planking from the guards, to put under their straw and keep them off the damp sand. Good. It would be a terrible risk but he was now determined to attempt it. His sanity and life depended upon it.

When the trapdoor flew open and the guard called, "Everybody up for exercise!" Byam stayed where he was.

One by one the wretched prisoners toiled up the slippery ladder. The guard counted them off. The tally didn't come out right. One man was missing. The guard put his head through the opening and yelled at Byam.

"Come on, you! Or I'll leave you down there for a week!"

Byam started to giggle idiotically. Then he stood up and began to cavort in his chains and he called the guard names and laughed about it.

"Another one gone mad," the guard said. He slammed the trapdoor shut.

Quickly now, Byam dropped his idiot act and hobbled over to the straw pallets of his fellow prisoners. He gathered up three six-foot planks and, half-stepping in his restricting chains, went down the beach and placed them in the water.

The planks didn't have much buoyancy, being somewhat waterlogged from the damp sand and moist straw. Byam clanked back to the beds and found more boards. Then he tore his rotting blanket into long strips and lashed all the planks together like a bundle of flat sticks.

At first he tried to sit on them but they sank under him. It was impossible to try to straddle them like a horse because of the length of chain between his ankles.

So he would have to immerse himself in the cold water and simply hang on to the makeshift raft as if it were a floating log.

He waded into the water, pushing his little raft ahead of him, and draped his chained arms and upper chest over it. He shoved off with his feet and started paddling with his hands.

It was exceedingly awkward. His weighted legs were of no use to him whatsoever; they simply sank and hung straight down. The best he could do was dog-paddle with his chained hands, making short chopping splashes at the water.

It only took a moment to get out of the light of the braziers, and then he was adrift on the wide, black stagnant pool. He didn't mind the chill of the water at first because his body had become accustomed to cold in the cavern; and he was too excited right at that moment to think of anything except escape. And now was the time of decision.

Which tunnel should he take?

It could well be a case of heads you win, tails I lose; but he had to make up his mind. He had committed himself body and soul to escape. He would take the farthest tunnel, the one on his right.

He paddled toward it slowly, the rock-ribbed wall looming out of the gloom like the sheer face of a mighty cliff. Then he was in the passage, and total darkness closed in on him like a clenched hand in a black glove.

The only sounds were the splashing of his hands and chains and the drippity-drip of the moist walls. He paddled along cautiously, feeling like a blind man in a dark room, looking for a black hat that wasn't there.

The right end of the raft bumped against rock. He hesitated indecisively, then swung to the left and paddled again. He seemed to be groping around a bend in the blind tunnel.

Again the raft struck — more violently this time — and he almost lost his clutch on it. Frightened now, he reached out and felt the slimy wall. He raised his hands and they stopped with a jar only a foot above his head.

The ceiling was only a matter of inches from the surface of the scummy water. If he tried to go on he would be squeezed under the black water. The right tunnel was the wrong tunnel. He was in a *cul-de-sac*.

He tried to turn the six-foot raft. The right end clobbered against rock. He swung it to the left and the same thing happened. Panic started to squirm up his water-numbed spine. His dragging legs were like lead. He trembled violently with the cold and started backing out of the tunnel, pushing at the chill wall and ceiling with his fettered hands.

He was at the point of exhaustion by the time he regained the great pool. Obviously there was only one course left open. He would have to try the left tunnel.

Tomorrow, he thought weakly. *I'll try it tomorrow.*

Then he realized that tomorrow was out of the question. It would take him too long to paddle back to the beach and replace the planks under the straw beds. It was almost time for the prisoners to return to their hole. He couldn't trust them; any one of them might inform on him just to gain extra privileges.

He started paddling toward the left-hand tunnel.

The thing that worried him now was that the prisoners would return and either see or hear him splashing at the far end of the pool and set up a howl about it. Through sheer determination of will he gathered up a strength he never knew he had and redoubled his efforts to gain the other tunnel.

He reached the yawning black mouth just as the prisoners started clanking and clattering down the iron ladder.

Again he was swallowed by darkness, but he kept at it, blindly, frantically — until the raft blundered around a bend in the tunnel. He stopped, sagging in the cold water with fatigue, gasping for breath. Then he became conscious of a very strange thing.

He was sweating.

He had not once sweated since the day he had been led into the mine sixteen months ago. The realization gave him a sense of courage and strength. He was still a human being. He could still direct the course of his own fate. He started paddling again.

"Byam! John Byam! Where are you?"

The questioning voices of the prisoners followed him like ghostly echoes. Then they diminished and all he heard was the splashing of his hands and the *drip drop* of the porous walls.

Would they start to howl like witless men in a crazy-house? Would the guards make an inquiry and take a count of heads? A sense of desperation swept over him and he pawed wildly at the water, penetrating deeper and deeper into the black tunnel.

He had to get out, had to get out, had to get —

One end of the raft struck a sudden projection of

rock. His momentum was so great that the raft tipped like a seesaw and swung around. Byam lost his equilibrium and his clutch and toppled into the water.

The weighty chains pulled him down. He fought them, springing to the surface spewing water and making a blind grab for the raft.

It came apart in his numb hands. The strain was too much for the rotting wrappings of the blanket. He felt the soggy boards drifting off in divergent directions. He couldn't hold them together. He started to sink.

His weighted feet struck bottom. He couldn't believe it. He stood up and a cold draft of air fanned across his wet face. That draft could come from only one place: the outlet.

He started wading and immediately the water deepened. By inches it crept up to his chin. But he couldn't stop now because he was certain he was going in the right direction. He was wading into the draft.

The water slid over his chin, then up to his mouth. He tilted his head back and kept on going. It was like wading into a nightmare. He was totally blinded by the inky dark. The water worked up to his nose. The chains pulled at him. He stumbled, went under, shoved up and clutched at the rock wall for support. And, for a moment, his nerve faltered.

Go on, he told himself. *You'll drown if you try to go back. So you might as well go on.*

He took a hobble-step forward, closing his eyes like a man stepping off a cliff to his death.

The water dropped to his chin, to his throat, and he felt the draft on his breastbone. He yelled *HA!* He couldn't help himself. He sucked a breath and waded on. The water shrank to his waist and the draft blew over his upper body.

He bumped fullfront into an obstacle. Feeling with his hands he found that the tunnel had graduated in size until it was no more than four feet high. The water was down to his ankles and it was flowing forward.

Stooping over, he entered the culvertlike passage and started groping. Claustrophobia was hugging him but he could not stop. The end was near now — but what the end would be he could not guess. He refused to think about it.

Suddenly a smear of light appeared on the water ahead. It *had* to be daylight! The tunnel was becoming a regular culvert now and he had to drop to his hands and knees. He crawled on, thrashing along like an animal on all fours.

A bend in the tunnel was coming. He splash-crawled around it frantically. And then — miraculously — he saw an orange-red glint of autumn some distance ahead.

But there was a grill between himself and the outer world.

He crawled toward it, hating it, growling in his throat like an outraged dog. He had gone through so much — and now this! Halting just inside the grill he looked out at the Halloween-dappled woods beyond. Freedom was waiting out there only one inch away.

His manacled hands came up and grabbed one of the lower struts. It was not iron. *The grill was made of wood.*

Gathering up his flagging strength, he threw himself bodily against the wooden grill. It was weather-rotten and it flew apart with a rending crackle. Byam toppled down a short, wet slope and sprawled out on his stomach.

He was out and he was free.

That same day he found a deserted blacksmith forge in the shed of an isolated farm and he struck off his irons. Then he started down the long path to Canada.

I have not been able to discover what happened to John Byam (his name is fictitious; his story is not) after his escape from Simsbury. I believe he joined one of the Tory regiments and fought against the American army for the remainder of the war.

CHAPTER 4

Like a Thief in the Night

MANY historians refer to Jack Sheppard as the prince of escapers, and several novelists and playwrights have endeavored to build young Jack into a carefree, witty, dashing and super-athletic romantic hero.

Certainly he was audacious and clever — but the unvarnished truth is, Jack Sheppard was a sneak thief.

Born in 1702, in Stepney, near London, Jack was brought up in the Bishopsgate workhouse, which was a sort of filth- and hunger-ridden poor people's detention hall in the eighteenth century. Certainly not the best environment for a young boy without parental guidance.

Apprenticed to a carpenter at an early age, Jack ran away when he was nineteen and took up with Bess Lyon (known as Edgeworth Bess among the London riffraff) and other shady slum characters. He immediately embarked upon a life of petty crime.

Jack's fame comes from his series of remarkable escapes — not from his ability as a thief. The fiction writers who later created a Robin Hood image of him completely overlooked the bald fact that he stole mostly spoons from darkened houses, used clothing from shuttered shops, and an occasional purse from an unguarded coat. He smacked far more of the lowly pickpocket than the glamorous highwayman.

But escape was Jack's special field.

Arrested twice in 1723, he broke out of the local jail both times and returned to his dubious haunts in glory. When his girl friend Bess was apprehended and placed in the St. Giles police station, Jack broke *into* the jail and freed her. His criminal companions now considered him to be quite the clever and daring fellow.

In May of 1724 both Jack and Bess were arrested and placed in the dreaded Newgate Prison. The same night Jack not only effected his own release but managed to carry off Miss Lyon as well. It was, up to that time, the most audacious escape ever made out of Newgate, and all the slum thieves hailed Jack's exploit as ingenious. Even the newspapers began to spread his reputation as an escape artist.

At this point Jack made the mistake of joining forces with Jonathan Wild — a receiver of stolen goods. Wild, unknown to his fellow thieves, was a police informer and he knew that a reward was being offered for his partner's arrest. On July 23, Wild turned the notorious Sheppard over to the law.

Jack's trial took place in Old Bailey on August 14. Thieves, even petty thieves of his sort, were dealt with harshly in that period; Jack was sentenced to death on the gallows, and was returned to Newgate to await execution.

It was the tightest spot he had yet been in, but Chance was still on his side. Bess Lyon smuggled a file in to him and Jack made his fourth spectacular escape.

All of London was agog with young Sheppard's exploits and a heavy reward was placed on his head. Jack stayed carefully under cover for the most part, but he carried two loaded pistols with him at all times and everyone said there would be violence if the law attempted to arrest him.

They were wrong. He was recognized by a Newgate jailer on September 10 and traced to a lodging house in Finchley. The house was immediately surrounded by armed police, and he was captured in bed and hauled off to Newgate.

This led to Jack Sheppard's most famous escape.

The prison officials went to some lengths to see that Jack did not vanish again. He was put into Newgate's strongest cell, known as "the Castle." It had double iron doors and a barred window too small for any human to squirm through. The precious prisoner was handcuffed and then manacled with heavy leg irons which were chained to a staple in the stone floor.

His execution had already been set for November 16, 1724.

Outwardly, Jack sat quietly and submissively in his chains in the lonely cell; but inwardly one dominant idea throbbed incessantly: Escape!

The Sessions began at Old Bailey in mid-October and most of Newgate's jailers were kept busy in court at that time. Jack was aware of it and he laid his plans accordingly, knowing that his harassed guards would have little time to spare for cell inspection.

At two o'clock in the afternoon of October 15 — right after his guard had brought him his food, checked his chains and departed — Jack Sheppard took the first step in the historic escape that would place his name in encyclopedias for centuries to come.

The physiological factor was in his favor. He was only five foot four and slender; the handcuffs were loose on his wrists. Clamping between his teeth the chain that connected the cuffs, he squeezed his fingers tightly together and pulled his hands down and through the manacles. It cost him some skin, but the cuffs were off.

He twisted the ankle-chain around and around and, with all his strength and the right pressure in the right place, snapped the central link which was secured to the staple in the floor. Pulling off his stockings, he ran the anklets as far up his shins as possible and tied the chains to his legs to prevent them from clattering and tripping him.

There was a fireplace in the cell, but when he looked up the chimney he saw it was guarded by an iron bar some distance up. Unlike Baron Trenck and Latude, who had endless months in which to contemplate their plans and set them in methodical operation, Jack had to decide and act on the spur of the moment.

He decided to make a hole in the chimney wall large enough for him to crawl through and to remove the obstacle. His only tool was the broken link of the ankle-chain but it had a sturdy, sharp end. He started picking with it just above the mantel.

The outer covering was plaster, but underneath the wall was made of mortised brick. His tool was small and unwieldy and it was going to be the devil's own job to remove even one brick. But he had no choice; the chimney was the only possible exit from the cell.

The first brick came loose. Delighted with his success he dug in with renewed energy, and within an hour he was standing ankle-deep in a dusty heap of bricks and mortar. He tried squirming into his hole and found that he could just do it. The iron bar was only a foot above his head.

He attacked the wall again. It was as rotten as old cheese inside the chimney and he pulled down chunk after chunk, ignoring the danger of having a heavy brick fall on his head and not pausing to think that some jailer might hear the noise of the falling rubble which he was dumping on the floor of the cell.

Half an hour later, and half stifled by the dense clouds of dust he had created, he had a hole three feet wide by six high. Now he was able to get a firm two-handed grip on the iron bar and exert the proper leverage against it. The ends were mortised between the bricks and he wrenched it loose without much trouble.

He climbed down to the littered cell to inspect his prize.

It was a square bar, a yard long and more than an inch thick. Compared to the inadequate little chain link the bar looked like the grandest tool in the world. He knew that ultimately he would have to escape by way of the roof and in order to get there he would have to pass through a number of locked doors. The iron bar would make an excellent jimmy.

His plan now was to break into the room over his cell by way of the chimney. He did some rapid calculation: His cell was eight feet high; add two more feet for the timbered stone floor above — ten; his hole was five feet above the hearth. Good! He would commence the upper hole five feet above the lower one.

He scrambled over the heap of rubbish and into the chimney and set to work vigorously. But it was a mean job. He was cramped and couldn't get the leverage he needed, and it was as dark as the inside pocket of a black cloak, and the mortar and soot dust nearly suffocated him.

Standing on the uneven edge of the lower hole on the tips of his aching toes, sweating and blinking and coughing in the sooty trash that rained on his head, he gouged and grouted and finally managed to punch out the first brick. He peered through the hole.

This upper cell was called the Red Room (its walls had once been painted that garish color) and it contained neither prisoners nor furniture. It was used for state prisoners and had not been occupied since 1716.

Jack started on the other bricks, ramming them into the Red Room as he loosened them, until he had removed nearly twenty. He pitched the bar into the empty room and hauled himself up the sooty wall and through the jagged hole, feeling vastly relieved to be out of the confining chimney.

A long rusty nail pricked his foot as he crossed the room and he picked it up for future use; any sort of tool was welcome. The Red Room's door was locked but he soon prised off the lockplate with his bar, slipped his fingers through the small hole and drew the outer bolt. He stepped into a dark clammy corridor.

The doors on the left led down to the King's Bench Ward and the Stone Ward and he could hear a murmur of voices floating up from them. He tiptoed to the end of the passage and was confronted with a heavy locked door. He ran his hand over it in the dark. The lock was on *the other side!*

He tried to jimmy the door with his bar but it was no use. Then he started to dig a hole through the wall nearest to the lock. Stubborn work. The wall was made of thick stone and the noise he created might possibly reach the ears of the prisoners in the Stone Ward. No help for it; it was either open this door or hang.

In half an hour he had made a hole just large enough for his arm. He reached through and fumbled around on the other side until his nerveless fingers touched the bolt. By joggling it up and down he was able to slip it back. The door swung open and he found himself in the prison chapel.

The chapel was divided into grilled pens and was used by the felons and debtors. Jack was standing in the felons' cage which was enclosed by an iron grating surmounted by iron spikes. It had a gate that was locked but he quickly jimmied it open with the bar, and then he entered the condemned pew.

This large circular pen was directly beneath the pulpit and prisoners condemned to death were brought here to hear their final sermon. Jack himself had sat on one of those benches only a short time before, and now he took his same seat again to catch a moment's rest.

Suddenly he felt haunted — as if he could actually hear the chaplain delivering the sermon for the condemned once again, urging him to prepare his tarnished soul for eternity. He stood up with a start and hurried over to the gate on the south side of the chapel.

Using his bar dexterously he snapped off one of the spikes surmounting the gate and scrambled over it, wiggling through the gap he had made in the iron teeth. He took the broken spike along just in case.

He trotted up a pitchy flight of steps which placed him in another cold corridor; and again he encountered a locked door. This made the fifth, counting the two pen gates in the chapel.

To his dismay he discovered that this door was secured with a strong, stubborn lock. It would not jimmy, he could not prise off the plate, nor could he pick the lock with the rusty nail he had been saving.

It cost him another half-hour of severe labor to gouge out the entire lockbox. He pushed and the door swung outward. Surely it would open onto the roof. He stepped forward in eager anticipation — and blundered against door number six!

It was greatly disheartening, and a brief inspection

of the obstacle made it more so. Running his hands over the bolted and barred surface he realized that the door was a masterpiece of resistance. All of the prison architect's craft seemed to have centered on this one accursed door.

The oak itself must have been as thick as a wall and it was crisscrossed with bolted iron bars. The lock was strongly plated, a foot wide, and fixed to the door with thick iron hoops. Below that a long sturdy bolt was shot into the socket and fastened to the hasp by a huge padlock. And instead of the usual wooden door jamb a seven-foot high, seven-inch wide, two-inch thick iron band was bolted to the doorpost. This was the housing for the bolt socket and the tongue of the lock. The hinges were set on the door on the outside and there was no way of getting to them.

His strength was already worn ragged, and now his spirit began to fail him. He slumped to the floor in a deep mood of dejection, half inclined to call it quits. That oak and iron-ribbed obstacle was enough to daunt any escaper.

Then he remembered that he was not just *any* escaper. He was Jack Sheppard, the twenty-two year old prince of escapers!

His spirit revived and he went at the door with his tools and determination. At the end of a brutal hour of sweat and strained muscles he had broken the nail and bent the bar but he had not made a dent in the mighty door.

Impossible! He couldn't get through; he was certain of it.

Gasping with fatigue, his hands so raw he could hardly hold his tools, he sagged against the wall thinking that he would willingly part with years of liberty for just one drink of water.

His brain reeled in his feverish head and for a vivid moment panic sparked him. He was certain he could hear the sound of footsteps coming rapidly toward him!

He was in a *cul-de-sac!* No exit! No way to turn!

He got a grip on himself, on his ragged nerves. His mind had tricked him; there were no footsteps. Regaining his self-possession he turned back to the weighty problem of the locked door.

Presently it occurred to him that he had been working on the wrong part of the barrier. Instead of fighting the door he should attempt to loosen the thick iron band on the doorpost. It was worth a try.

Prying with the spike, shoving with the bar, he managed to get the end of the bar between the iron band and the jamb. Then, with one foot against the doorpost and throwing the rest of his weight into the lever, he slowly pried the iron fillet loose.

It took a full backbreaking hour to lever the entire band away from the doorpost, but when it came free it brought the bolt socket and the lockbox with it. He passed through the doorway, went up a few steps to door number seven, which was bolted on the inside, opened it and stepped out on the roof.

He was breathing fresh air and all of London was sprawled at his feet.

The flat roof was shingled with lead and was joined

to the battlements of one of the gate towers. Jack followed some wooden steps up to the eighth door. It was locked. He could have pried it open but by now he was growing concerned over the time. It was already dark, and a jailer just might look into his cell.

He returned to the seventh door and climbed it, reached for the edge of the wall above and pulled himself up.

At that moment the clock of St. Sepulchre gonged eight times. He was now on the upper roof of Newgate and it had taken him six hours to get there from his cell.

Running along the wall he climbed over the upper battlements and lowered himself to the roof of the gate, and then he scrambled over the parapets to the north tower and on down to a lower roof which faced Giltspur Street. The flat roof of a house loomed out of the darkness directly below his position. He stared at it longingly.

The sheer drop appeared to be about twenty feet.

He took a quick cast about, looking for a more advantageous place to attempt a descent, but could find nothing better. He stalled indecisively. He might very easily break a thigh or something worse if he jumped, which would leave him helpless and open to capture. So —

He didn't want to do it but he had no alternative. He would have to go all the way back to his cell for his blanket, to make a rope. A risky business; his absence might have been noticed by this time. He took along the iron bar in case he bumped into a jailer.

Back across the roofs, the battlements, down the

stairs, along the black corridors and through the doors he had broken open, he passed hurriedly through the great empty chapel — and heard someone singing and other voices laughing.

Reassuring sounds. If his escape *had* been detected the excitement of the hue and cry would be ringing through the old prison, not song and laughter.

Slipping into the Red Room he climbed down the chimney and returned to his cell. His blanket was buried under the mound of rubble and he had to dig the heap away to get at it. Then he had to retrace his long dark passage back to the roof overlooking Giltspur Street.

He tore the blanket into wide strips, knotted them together and tied one end to the spike which he hammered into the mortar with his bar. Then he went over the edge and lowered himself down the side of the prison and dropped gently onto the flat roof.

Crouching like a hunted fox, he listened and looked and spotted a garret door in the roof. It was unlocked and he slipped into an inky bedroom. Just as he reached the inner door one of his leg chains slipped.

Clickety-clank!

"Oh Lor! What's that?" a woman's voice cried out from her bed.

Jack froze with his hand on the doorknob.

"Only the cursed dog," a man's voice growled. "Go to sleep."

Jack let out his breath and stole down the stairs.

He had almost gained the hall when a door swung open and the maid and her gentleman caller stepped out with a lighted candle. Jack dodged into the first doorway he found and blundered across the dark room and into a screen. He slipped behind it and waited with his heart hammering violently.

The voices of the maid and her caller droned on and on in the hall, until finally Jack heard the door creak open — then shut. The glow of the candle disappeared and Jack crept out of hiding, into the hall, out the front door, and found himself in the deserted street.

It was midnight when he passed the watchman at St. Sepulchre, and he said, "Good evening, sir," and turned into Gray's Inn Lane.

After wandering through the gardens south of Euston Road he entered the fields near Tottenham Court and took shelter in a cowshed. It was three A.M. when he fell soundly asleep.

He was awakened at seven in the morning by a heavy downpour drumming on the leaky roof of the shed. The sad truth was, he didn't know what to do next. He was still wearing the leg irons and had no way of removing them, and he was afraid he wouldn't be able to conceal them in the daylight.

Night came and the rain continued. His hunger prompted him to go to a tawdry little shop in Tottenham Road where he purchased some bread and cheese. When he attempted to buy a hammer and chisel from the proprietress he was met with a blank refusal. He slunk back to the cowshed for the night.

The next day was Saturday and it was still raining.

Jack was growing frantic. He couldn't remain indefinitely in the stinking cowshed, yet he couldn't cut and run as long as he was hamstrung by the clattering leg irons. He thought of approaching the neighborhood blacksmith, but rejected the idea. The smith would likely turn him in for the reward.

Sunday came. In his desperation he tried to pound his anklets into an oblong shape with a heavy stone, hoping to be able to slip them over his heels. It didn't work — but a casual passerby heard the noise he was making and looked into the shed.

"What on earth are you doing here, and why are you wearing those irons?" the man asked.

"I just escaped from Bridewell," Jack invented rapidly. "I was imprisoned there because I couldn't pay a debt that some lying merchant lodged against me. Will you help me? I'll give you twenty shillings if you'll fetch a hammer and chisel."

The nameless man was a shoemaker and it is quite possible that he guessed Jack's true identity. If he did, he kept it to himself. He went away with the money and returned shortly with a hammer and a chisel. The shoemaker and the thief went to work on the irons.

Jack Sheppard had started his famous escape at two o'clock on Thursday afternoon. At five o'clock on Sunday afternoon he walked out of the cowshed a free man.

Jack Sheppard was audacious and clever, but he was not gifted with common sense. Instead of fleeing London while he had the chance, he made the mistake of hanging around his old haunts, basking in the glory of his remarkable escape. Eight days after he escaped from Newgate he was discovered by the police and captured.

He was executed on the gallows November 16, 1724, before an admiring crowd of 200,000 people, and was buried that night in the churchyard of St. Martin's-in-the-Fields. One hundred and forty-two years later some workmen who were digging the foundation for the new National Gallery discovered his coffin.

CHAPTER 5

The Unknown Fact

LATUDE and d'Aligre were not Madame de Pompadour's only prisoners. There was the young Breton noble Alaine Sieur de Kermen who wrote a witty verse about La Pompadour, and paid for it in a most tragic way.

Two days after the publication of his poem Kermen was hauled out of his home and escorted to an island off the Breton coast which was a sort of Alcatraz of a bygone age. In part it was a monastery under the charge of monks; but it also had a royal commandant and a garrison of soldiers who guarded the King's political prisoners.

It was France's most dreaded prison. Architects called it the Marvel; the people called it the Ocean Bastille; but on maps it was referred to as Mont St. Michel.

Twice a day when the tide went out Mont St. Michel was connected to the mainland by miles and miles of flat damp sand. When the tide came in this natural land bridge was buried under seventy feet of treacherous sea and the Mont became an isolated island. That was the situation at St. Michel when Kermen arrived in 1762, and it remains the same to this day.

The island itself was nothing but a great pile of bare

rock, and for centuries the Bretons had been plastering it over with seawalls, massive staircases, chapels, storerooms, guardrooms, cells and lofty towers. Kermen was conducted to a bastion halfway up the sprawling cluster of masonry.

Inside a large cell was a cage eight feet square. It had massive wooden bars two inches thick, hewn of oak. One end of the cage was pushed up against the cell's outer stone wall so Kermen could stare through his small Gothic window at the beauties of freedom outside.

His guard, a rather sinister man named Dupont, clamped the rusty padlock on Kermen's cage and grinned at him through the bars.

"This cage of yours is a final prison within the heart of a prison," he said mockingly. "You'll grow old and feeble in here, my friend."

"Not necessarily," Kermen said. "I have not yet been tried or sentenced. Perhaps I'll be freed sooner than you think."

Dupont laughed and said, "Pompadour's prisoners are never tried or sentenced — at least not in a court of law. *She* tries you, and the King sentences you for life."

For life! The bleak words threw a chill of despair over the young nobleman. Then his black-browed face hardened with resolution. Where there was a way in, there had to be a way out.

Dupont fetched him his food twice a day. The second time, at dusk, he let Kermen out of the cage and cell and allowed him a half-hour stroll on the bastion platform. He walked with him, of course, and it was his habit to tease the quiet prisoner about the prospects of escape from the Mont.

"It's quite impossible, you know. Even if you *could* get out of your cage you would still have to get out of the cell. Then there would be this bastion. It's 300 feet from here to the sands below and there are many heavily guarded walls in between. Then there is the sea itself. It goes in, it goes out. When it is in, you would drown. When it is out, you would find yourself caught in the quicksands. Well, do I tempt you?"

Kermen said nothing; but under his calm acceptance of destiny hid a clawing spirit. A way out — there had to be a way out for a man of resolution and determination. He looked out at the sands sprawling for miles around the islet. Those gleaming sands beckoned him to liberty.

It was August when he entered the Mont; September had come and gone, and now, October. Kermen laid his plans bit by bit, adding this, rejecting that; observing, studying, thinking. There was no hope of escape from his bastion by way of the staircase; too many gates, watchrooms and sentries on the walls below. On the other hand his bastion wall plunged straight down through a great gulf of emptiness to the foot of the Mont. No possible way of climbing down *that!*

And that was precisely the hinge of the entire problem: getting from the bastion to the sands. He could handle everything else with his own ingenuity.

During his daily walks he observed that the platform of his bastion joined a wing of the abbey buildings by way of a battlement approach. There were lower walls under those buildings but how to reach them from the abbey parapet? Then one day he heard a loud screaking noise and, looking around, he saw an interesting sight.

A large wheel and crane swung out over the kitchen roof of the nearest abbey building. A rope ran through the wheel and dropped straight down to the sands. Three men working the winch inside the kitchen were bringing up the Mont's supplies in a huge net.

Dupont noticed Kermen's interest and he smiled crookedly.

"Gives you ideas, eh Kermen? If boxes and barrels can come *up* on the rope — a man should be able to go down, *n'est-ce pas?*"

Kermen said nothing and Dupont chuckled.

"A prisoner tried that method once," he said tauntingly. "He didn't know that the men in the kitchen have to control the brake on the winch. Without the brake the rope, with a weight on it, drops like a rock. That's how the prisoner went down — all the way like a rock. But he was like a crushed egg when we found him at the foot of the Mont!"

Kermen turned away, still silent, and Dupont laughed mockingly. But inwardly Kermen was a jelly of nervous excitement. His biggest problem was solved. The rest would just take time.

Each day as he took his exercise he secretly studied the ramparts leading to the abbey kitchen and the height and configuration of the various walls below. He observed where each sentry made his rounds and concluded that only one of them would concern him directly — the guard on the kitchen roof.

From the little window in his cell he could see the mainland and he judged it was about a mile and a half from the Mont to the Breton coast. At night he could see the distant lights of the little town of Pontorson. Unfortunately, he could not see much of the sands or sea around the islet, but he knew that all commerce traveled a direct route over the bare sand from the main entrance of the Mont to Pontorson.

So — using the Mont's entrance as a starting point he had only to follow a straight course to Pontorson's lights in order to avoid the quicksand traps. He knew nothing of the local conditions regarding the tide, but he did know it was universally accepted that from ebb tide to flood tide required six hours. The time and tide were very vital to his calculations.

He had help in keeping track of time; the sentinels never failed to call their hourly "All's well," and the abbey bells also tolled the hour. He learned to count the minutes between by using his own pulse beat.

The timing had to be exact. He had to time his escape from the cage, the cell, the bastion and the Mont so that when he reached the sands below he would have time to race to the mainland just ahead of the incoming tide. This would cut off any pursuit from the Mont. The sea itself would be his bulwark against recapture.

He removed a rusted iron clamp from his wooden bed frame and sharpened one end of it on the stones of the wall and then set to work on one of the thick wooden bars of his cage. It took time; the aged oak was like iron itself. He chiseled the bar down until it was held in place by a mere sliver of wood. He filled the notch with breadcrumb paste and dirt in order to hoodwink Dupont when he made his daily inspection of the cage.

Day and night his brain raked over each phase of his plans and calculations, taking care that he left no loophole for chance to trick him. He was certain he had neglected nothing, had overlooked no small detail that might wreck his plans.

The cold days and freezing nights of November and December passed, and then it was January. He set his escape for the night of the twenty-fifth. Promptly at eight o'clock he would remove the bar in his cage. From that point on everything was figured exactly and precisely, down to the smallest detail.

Success was assured. He was certain of it.

The long days inched up to the twenty-fifth. He showed no excitement, no impatience. His studied calm came from total self-confidence. He even took a nap in the afternoon, in order to be fresh for his escape that night.

At six o'clock Dupont brought him his food and escorted him to the platform for his walk. The tide was still out and the drying sands looked ominously gray in the gathering dusk. There was no fog (that was vital: he couldn't see Pontorson's lights in a fog) and no promise of a moon. Nothing but chill starlight.

Perfect! He had picked the ideal night.

Then the wheel of fate made a slight turn and one

of chance's spokes protruded into his plans. Dupont's lantern blew out and he brought it into the cell to relight it. The wick failed and he left it on the floor with a curse. When he had locked Kermen in his cage for the night, he walked out of the cell forgetting the lantern.

Kermen instantly saw the danger. Dupont might remember about the lantern and return to the cell for it later on — probably right in the middle of Kermen's break.

"Dupont!" he called after him. "You forgot your lantern. I'll not need it when I leave here tonight, so you may as well take it along."

Dupont scoffed at the absurdity of Kermen's leaving the prison that night or any night. He picked up his lantern and departed laughing. Kermen smiled in the dark. The unexpected had happened and he had been equal to it. He congratulated himself. The incident seemed like a good omen.

He ate his meal and remained sitting on his cot in the dark, resolved not to make a move toward escape until the proper moment. Now that the time was very near the suspense of waiting became an agony. But he restrained himself, listening for the voices of the sentries.

Dupont had departed at seven. Kermen counted the sixty minutes on his pulse beat; then the call from the guard on the kitchen roof — "Eight o'clock and all's well round my post!"

It was time. He moved quickly and methodically in the dark. He had rehearsed every moment over and over and could have done what he had to do wearing a blindfold. Wrapping his hands about the notched cage bar he exerted pressure and it broke off — a two foot length of seasoned oak, two inches thick.

He turned to the cage door. The rusty iron padlock was as old as the cage, which dated back to Louis XI; some three hundred years. He placed the notched end of his lever against it just so and put his weight on it. The entire lock broke apart like a rotten shell. Kermen stepped out of the cage and over to the cell door.

The cell lock was set in the wooden door and would have to be pried apart. He was prepared. Using a section of his bedframe for a fulcrum he inserted the sharpened end of the bar in the jamb and wrenched the whole affair loose.

He already knew there was no outer bar on the door, and so he swung it open for a look along the corridor, and then closed it. Every nerve in his body started to tingle with the impulse to break and run, but he held himself back. Timing, perfect timing was the key to a successful escape.

Quite deliberately he returned to the cage and sat down on his cot to wait for the right moment.

The cell was bitter cold with winter drafts but Kermen sat in a nervous sweat. He knew that the sands around the Mont were dry and if he could reach them now he would be able to gain the mainland without the slightest difficulty. But his plan held him waiting in the cage. The guard on the kitchen roof had to be eliminated at precisely nine o'clock. His removal would not be discovered by the other sentinels until ten, which would give Kermen one precious hour of free time.

Seconds, minutes, time beat in his pulse. Then the abbey bell gonged the end of hospice. It was eight-thirty. He concentrated on his pulse beats. *Eight-thirty-five . . . forty . . . forty-five . . . eight-fifty.* He picked up his bar and walked out of the cage and cell, along the corridor and stepped out on the platform.

Staying in the shadows of the wall he crossed the ramparts to the kitchen roof and crouched in the angle of a buttress. The sentry was pacing his post in the chill starlight, passing Kermen's dark nook on every other turn.

Then, from the lower ramparts, came the string of hourly calls from the other sentries, passing from guard to guard, on up to the kitchen roof. The sentry paused with his back to Kermen and gave his call.

"Nine o'clock and all's well round my post!"

Barefooted, Kermen slipped up behind him and raised his heavy bar. *Thomp!* and the guard was dead at his feet, his head crushed. Kermen took the man's crossbelts and swordbelt and his musket and bayonet, and hurried across the parapet to the spot directly over the kitchen window.

The huge protruding crane was ten feet below.

Buckling the belts together he secured them to a projection on the parapet and, using the leather loops as a rope, lowered himself until his feet rested on the top of the crane.

Balanced precariously, clinging to the belts with one hand, he reached down with the fixed bayonet on the musket and tried to catch the rope that ran through the wheel and went into the kitchen window below.

Treacherous gusts of wind whipped around him, and his straining arms began to tingle with warning pain. He was teetering above a sheer, tremendous gulf, stretching his body farther and farther. If he slipped, if the belts gave way, he would be gone in one long deadly plunge.

Twice the bayonet had the rope, only to let it slip over the point. He reached again — the bayonet caught the rope — raised it slightly and began to draw it. The wheel creaked and, slowly, the rope started to come up to him — coming from the window where it lay on the kitchen floor in a great coiled mound.

Carefully he inched his hand along the musket, balancing it and the weight of the rope, until his fingers reached the rope and gripped it.

Giddy with vertigo he pulled himself back to the parapet and sagged limply over the edge, clutching the rope securely in his hand.

He pulled up yard after yard of the stout, flexible rope until he had as much as he could carry. Then he sawed through it with the bayonet, shouldered the huge coil and went along the rampart to a lower abbey roof. Securing one end to a projection he lowered the rope down — down — until it reached the soldiers' garden beside the giant staircase leading down from the abbey to the lower walls.

The staircase itself was unguarded but he knew that sentries were posted along the lower walls which rose straight up from the foot of the Mont. Great caution must be exercised at this point.

Returning to the parapet over the crane he hauled up another fifty or sixty yards of rope, lugged it back to the projection, tied the musket to one end and let it down to the garden below. Then he eased himself over the edge, grasped the first rope firmly and began to let himself down the tremendous height.

He moved mechanically, as he would have done if he had been coming down before friends in broad daylight to win a wager. But it was not easy. The black yawning void under him was unnerving. He banged against the stone wall, burned his hands on the coarse rope, and halfway down the strength in his arms began to fail him.

He slipped, grasped, swung dizzily; the rough stones rasped at his clothes and skin; an agonizing stab of pain knifed between his shoulders which took his breath away; the rope would not remain stationary but undulated constantly, swinging him away from the wall — into the wall —

He went down the last ten feet in a dropping rush and fell on an acacia in the soldiers' garden. He was unhurt except for his raw bleeding hands.

Quickly gathering up his loose second rope he hurried across the garden to the abbey staircase. His legs were all rubbery as if stuffed with wadding, and his strength after five months of close confinement was merely the strength of nervous energy.

Placing himself boldly between two sentries not far from each other and both clearly visible to him in the starlight, he began to disentangle the second rope and lay it out on the curb of the stairs. He could hear the guards talking close by and he was resolved to stab the first one who came near him with the bayonet.

Again his iron will took command of his agitation and he worked on the tangle of rope as though he were performing a mute ceremony. Aside from the minor discomfort of bleeding hands, everything was falling out as he had planned. No alarm had been given and he was halfway down the Mont with no broken bones.

With the carefully coiled rope over his shoulder, he slipped along the wall of the towers until he reached the outer face of battlements. A sentry was pacing his post less than fifty yards away.

Kermen waited until the man's back was turned and then he darted out and fastened his rope in an opening in the parapet, made for rainwater to run through, dumped the coil over the edge to slither out on its own weight, and raced back to the shadows for cover.

Breathless, watching intently, he saw the sentry turn again at the edge of his round and start back. Kermen darted out of cover and ran barefooted to the parapet, slipped through the embrasure and was out of sight before the sentry faced about.

Scraping and swinging against the last and lower wall he did his best to cling to the naked stones, fearing his descent might be heard by the guard above.

A sudden sharp voice brought him to a trembling, clutching halt. Then he heard a low laugh float on the still night air and he relaxed. Two sentries had met on the parapet and were passing some private joke.

During the last half of his descent the outward slope of the wall was of great assistance to him. He could actually "walk" down part of it like a mountaineer, and the wild plants growing between the stones helped to hold him up. Then his sliding feet struck something solid.

He looked around. He was on the rocks below the walls. The vast acres of sands lay bare in the starlight. He climbed down the damp rocks and found himself standing on the sand.

Cage, cell, bastion, the Mont itself — all that was behind him. Now all he had to do was reach a point near the Mont's entrance, taking a bearing on Pontorson's distant lights and strike a straight course to safety and liberty!

He trotted around the rocks, taking a chance on the quicksands here; but luck was with him and the sand remained firm underfoot. Soon he found himself within one hundred feet of the Mont's lighted entrance, and he lined up his course with the twinkling village of Pontorson on the mainland.

He struck out for the far shore, going at an easy lope. Ahead of him and around him the starstruck sands stretched level and bare. He ran on into the night, the scattered lights of Pontorson beckoning him on and on, but never seeming to come closer.

He began to fear he had made a slight miscalculation. Perhaps Pontorson was *more* than a mile and a half from the Mont. Looking at it from above, as he had from his lofty platform on the bastion, might have foreshortened the actual distance. Now he suspected it was much more like two miles, maybe three.

But he had nothing to fear. Surely he had already

covered one mile if not more, and the flood tide was not due until ten o'clock which was still some minutes away; and everyone knew that an incoming tide gave plenty of warning and took nearly an hour to reach its flood point.

At this moment fate stepped in with a vengeance. Looking at the dark barren sands ahead of him, Kermen saw a river appear suddenly. Abruptly, and all around him, the night was filled with the gushing sound of water. The tide was rushing in on both sides!

He slammed to a halt, baffled and shocked. All his calculations had been based on the fact that it was six hours from ebb to flood tide. What he didn't know was that Mont St. Michel was one of the few places in the world *where the tide could rise to full flood within five minutes.*

Coming across miles of level sands the sea was suddenly filling the channels of unseen rivers, springing out of the porous sand itself. It came rushing and flooding at a breathtaking speed. Everywhere Kermen turned the black gray-topped water rumbled and crashed.

He saw that he could no longer reach Pontorson. The charging water cut him off. He changed his direction, running a few steps forward — then had to change it again as another tributary of the oncoming tide stopped him short.

He turned left — water breaking; he turned right — a sudden gushing among the starlit sands. He turned — turned — bewildered and frantic, and spotted an opening. He ran into it full tilt — anywhere to get out of that treacherous maze of sand and water.

Within six steps he felt the ground sag under his feet and he stumbled and fell and all at once he was knee-deep in wet sand. *Quicksand!*

He reached for an outcropping of sunbaked sand and it crumbled in his hand. He kicked with his feet and one foot swung free, but — as he took another desperate stride forward — both his feet sank into the sand that was suddenly like mush, and now he floundered helplessly, beating the porous sand with his hands.

He sank — sank — screaming and thrashing as the icy black water gurgled into the quicksand pit around him. More and more tons of cold dark sea rolled in and, a moment later, everything for miles around was water and there was the eternal lonely silence of the sea.

There is a legend that Kermen's pardon from the King arrived at Mont St. Michel the morning after he was lost in the tide. This sounds almost too ironic to be true.

CHAPTER 6

The Brink of Eternity

IN 1755 Casanova de Seingalt, the renowned Italian adventurer, was arrested by the Inquisition in Venice and imprisoned in the Doges' Palace, known as the Leads. He was not informed of the charge against him and could only surmise that one of his many enemies had turned him in as a spy or as a dabbler in black magic.

Knowing what we do of Casanova it was probably a case of "if the shoe fits, wear it." So Casanova was wearing it but he resolved it wouldn't be for long. Escape was uppermost in his mind.

The prison was called the Leads because of its lead-plated roof, and Casanova's first cell was an old lumber room in the attic. It suited him fine. Among the clutter of odds and ends in the room he found a long iron bolt which he fashioned into a crowbar, and he set to work to dig a hole through the roof.

Then — the reversal of fortune. The thing that had happened to Baron Trenck happened to Casanova. Just as he was prepared to make his break the jailers walked in.

"We now have a regular cell prepared for you, signore. A fine bright room, from which you will be able to see half of Venice."

Casanova protested that he didn't want to see half of Venice. He *loved* the lumber room. He wanted to stay where he was. But no — the chief jailer, Lorenzo, ordered his removal to the floor below.

Passing through the spacious attic he had an opportunity to glance into another room. Two prisoners occupied the cell along with a great clutter of old books. It gave Casanova an inspiration. He had money for personal necessities and he gave some to Lorenzo to buy him some books. The jailer had no objection.

Even though he still had the crowbar hidden in his clothes he knew he would not be able to escape from his new cell without assistance, so he made a pretense of reading hurriedly through the books Lorenzo had purchased for him. He had learned that the two men in the cell directly over his were the Friar Balbi and the Count Asquino, and that it was the friar who was the great reader.

Selecting a random book Casanova penned a Latin motto in one of the margins: *Calamitosus est animus futuri anxius* — Wretched is the man who is anxious about the future. Then he called for Lorenzo.

"I've read all my books and desire more. I would like to lend this one to Friar Balbi. Bring me one of his in exchange."

The next day Lorenzo brought him one of the friar's books, and to his great delight Casanova found a note between the pages. The friar stated that he was ripe for escape but had no idea how to go about it.

In another book Casanova wrote that he had a plan. If he could find a way to smuggle his crowbar to the

THE BRINK OF ETERNITY

Casanova

friar, the friar could then cut a hole in the floor of his cell and Casanova would climb through it. Once in the attic again he vowed he would succeed in freeing all three of them.

The rub was, how to smuggle the crowbar?

Communicating back and forth with their books, Casanova began to grow apprehensive over the wild suggestions the good friar offered concerning the transportation of the crowbar. Some of his ideas were downright harebrained, and Casanova started to suspect that the man was addled. However, it was the dimwitted friar or no one.

Casanova was allowed to prepare his meals in his cell and he requested that Lorenzo bring him the biggest platter in the Leads.

"I intend to make a macaroni dinner for the two gentlemen in the cell above," he explained, "to celebrate St. Michael's day."

Selecting his Bible, a large folio book, he slipped the crowbar inside it. The Bible was eighteen inches long, which left an inch of crowbar sticking out at either end; but the macaroni platter was two feet long.

Calling for Lorenzo, he placed the steaming platter on top of the Bible and handed the whole affair to the jailer, saying:

"The Bible is a special gift for the friar."

It worked. Friar Balbi received the bar and started to dig a hole under his bed.

A week passed and no hole appeared in Casanova's ceiling. The friar wrote to complain that the floor was solid brick and he was having a devil of a time. Another week of anxious waiting; more complaints from Balbi; then more and more days, until Casanova was ready to tear his hair. What was the idiot friar doing?

Finally on October 30, Casanova heard a stamping on the floor above — a prearranged signal meaning that the friar was ready to break through the floor.

Casanova hastily wrote in a book: *Tomorrow at noon. Prepare a rope tonight.* And sent Lorenzo up with the message.

That same afternoon a disreputable looking rogue called Soradaci was thrust into his cell with the announcement that he was to be Casanova's cellmate!

Casanova was appalled. He needed only one look at the sly-faced creature to know that the man was a police spy. And it had to happen on the very eve of his escape!

What to do? If Soradaci learned of the proposed escape he would immediately inform Lorenzo, and that would kick all their plans into a cocked hat. After questioning the rogue at some length Casanova came to the conclusion that the man was simple-minded and inordinately superstitious.

"Look here," he said harshly, "I believe you are an informer."

Soradaci protested excitedly, but Casanova wouldn't listen.

"You know that I am Casanova de Seingalt, the famous black magician, and you know that I have infernal powers. I am now going to remove you from this earth to keep you from spying on me!"

Horrified, the gullible Soradaci fell to his knees and begged Casanova not to strike him dead with his devilish arts. Casanova pretended to think about it.

"Very well," he agreed. "I will let you live for the moment. *But* — to show you that it is within my power to do what I threaten, I will call down the Angel of Death precisely at noon tomorrow. If at that time you do not do my bidding — I will send you away with Death!"

Fantastic as it may seem, the poor superstition-ridden Soradaci actually swallowed this incredible threat. He was dead certain that Casanova could and would bring down the avenging Angel of Death!

It was a sleepless night for both of them; Soradaci in his trembling fear and Casanova in sweating anxiety. Morning found Soradaci cringing in a corner, staring apprehensively at the ceiling. Casanova also watched the ceiling as he paced the cell.

Eleven o'clock . . . twelve . . . *thump thump* on the floor above.

"Listen!" Casanova hissed. "The Angel of Death comes!"

A wide circle of plaster dropped from the ceiling and Friar Balbi's bald head appeared in the hole. "Are you ready, my son?"

Poor Soradaci fell to the floor whimpering for mercy. Casanova kicked the wretch to his feet and ordered him to climb through the hole and not make a sound. A minute later Casanova was in the upper cell embracing Friar Balbi.

"Your task is done," he said, "and now mine begins."

"Count Asquino is too sick to attempt an escape," Balbi told him, and Casanova went over to see the invalid nobleman.

"Your plan is too rash to succeed with a fool like Balbi and a rogue like Soradaci," the count warned him.

"That may be, signore, but I intend to go on step by step to liberty or death. We will leave Soradaci here in your care. But we need money and I have none."

Unfortunately the count was an avaricious man and he would loan Casanova only two sequins (about $4.50). Then, to add to Casanova's irritation, he found that the lax Balbi had not made a rope. They wasted four hours in cutting up their sheets, blankets and mattress covers and knotting them into two 150-foot ropes. On top of everything else Friar Balbi turned troublesome, complaining that Casanova had deceived him.

"You said your scheme was complete, but it is not so. All we have accomplished thus far is to get you out of your cell."

Ignoring him, Casanova set to work with the crowbar

to make a hole in the eaved roof. The rafters were easy enough but the outer sheet of lead was riveted. He managed to detach it by thrusting the bar between the gutter and the sheet and using leverage, and then raising it like a trapdoor on his shoulders.

Sunset had already closed the day and a grinning moon was in its first quarter, which momentarily upset Casanova's plans. He intended to cross the palace roof and get down into St. Mark's Square; but now he knew that all of Venice would be out on the square on such a glorious moonlit night as this.

They had to wait for the moon to set, and it took the devil's own time to do it. It was well after eleven before the moon began to pale behind an encroaching fog. They bundled the ropes in their cloaks, bade the count farewell and climbed out on the roof. It had a treacherous slope and the leads were slippery with the damp mist. Casanova led the way on all fours.

He wedged the crowbar between the edges of the lead sheets, pried up a handhold and dragged himself foot by foot up to the ridge of the roof. The friar clutched him by the back of the belt which gave Casanova the double task of both dragging and carrying.

"My hat!" the friar whispered. "It fell over the edge!"

Casanova felt like giving him a kick and sending him after his cursed headgear. If some guard away down in the courtyard happened to notice that falling hat —

With immense difficulty they managed to reach the ridge and they straddled it to get their breath — and Balbi promptly dropped his bundle of rope. Dismayed, Casanova watched the bundled cloak roll down the roof and disappear over the edge; this time on the opposite side, into the canal.

"A bad omen," Balbi moaned.

"Stay where you are before you drop yourself," Casanova growled. "I will reconnoiter the roof and find us a way down."

In his straddled position he had to shuffle along the ridge like an inchworm. The night mist was deceptively dense now as he labored around the steep roof like a man astride a long timber over a vast foggy chasm. A slip to the right and he would roll down the leads and drop into the courtyard far below; a sudden tilt to the left and he would instantly plunge into the black canal. The canal was only three or four feet deep and it would mash him to pulp from this tremendous height.

He spent an hour in going about the roof, examining every corner in vain for something strong enough to attach the rope to. There was nothing; even the cupolas of the church of St. Mark, which was attached to the Doges' Palace, offered nothing except precipitous walls which he knew he had no hope of surmounting.

However, something had to be decided or dawn would catch him sitting up there on the ridge like a foolish toad on a log. He fastened his eye on a dormer window on the side toward the canal. It was far enough from the spot where he had left Balbi to make him think that it would open into a loft that belonged to the church rather than into the prison.

Letting himself slip carefully down the leads he was soon astride the dormer's little roof. Leaning over and reaching down, he was able to see and touch a barred grating with a small leadpaned window behind it. Unfortunately the dormer was right at the edge of the steep eaves and inaccessible in any way that would allow him to stand in front of it.

Drawing the crowbar from his belt and sprawling flat on the peaked roof, he wedged the bar above the frame of the grate and levered back on it with all his might. In fifteen minutes he had dislodged the grating and drawn it up to lean it against the side of the dormer. Then he jimmied open the little window.

With the help of the bar he reached the ridge of the roof and inched back to where he had left his companion. The friar was half wild with fear and anger.

"The foul fiend's curse on you for leaving me here by myself all this time!" he raged. Casanova smiled in the dark.

"What did you think had become of me?"

"I thought you had fallen down some roof or wall! What have you been doing all this time?"

"Come with me and you'll see."

They straddled back to the dormer where they were faced with a heavy problem. It would be easy for one man to get into the loft through the window because the other man could let him down on the rope; but how could the second man follow him when there was no way of securing the rope above the window? They had no way of knowing the height of the window above the floor of the loft, and if the second man climbed in and let himself drop to the floor without the rope he might very well break his legs.

"Let me down at any rate," the friar said selfishly,

"and when I am in there you will have plenty of time to find out how you can follow me."

Casanova's first impulse of indignation was to hit the self-seeking friar with the crowbar; but this rash emotion passed and he agreed to the suggestion. After all he *had* originally promised to find a way to free the friar, and he believed in living up to his bargain.

He tied the rope under Balbi's armpits, had him lie flat on his stomach with his feet outwards, and then let him down onto the roof of the dormer. The friar went over the edge and into the window as far as his hips, leaving his arms on the sill.

Casanova slipped down the leads and stretched himself face down on the little roof and, clutching the rope firmly, told Balbi to let himself go.

Yard after yard of rope slipped through Casanova's clenched hands as the vanished friar went slowly down into the loft. Reaching the floor Friar Balbi untied the rope and Casanova pulled it up, estimating the number of feet by the length between each knot.

Maladetto! The distance was *over fifty feet*. Far too great a height to risk a drop without a rope. The good friar, now feeling perfectly safe, called up an impractical suggestion.

"Throw in the rope and I'll take care of it. We might have need of it again!"

Casanova had need of it right then and there, though he didn't know how to put it to use. He ignored the friar's absurd demand. In desperation he crawled back to the ridge to explore farther along the chapel roof.

He came to a small platform which some workmen had erected by a cupola, and discovered a tub full of wet mortar and a ladder that was nearly fifteen yards long. The fickle hand of fate!

Tying the rope to the top rung he dragged the balky ladder back to the dormer. He then had to get the clumsy contraption *into* the window — which for a lone man straddling a little roof over a great deadly void was a Herculean task. Clutching the heavy, off-balanced object he tied the rope to the eighth rung and let it down until it was parallel with the window, and then he tried to jockey it through the small opening.

The ladder went in as far as the fifth rung and then the end caught against the inside slant of the dormer and no power on earth could budge it farther without breaking the ladder. He would have to tilt the outer end which would allow the ladder to slide in by its own weight.

He slid down the side of the dormer on his stomach until his toes found the gutter. Leaning out over space he joggled the ladder with one hand, up and down, up and down, and saw it slip in a foot farther. But he leaned too far . . .

All at once his toes slipped off the gutter and he dropped, and the next thing he knew he was dangling on the brink of eternity by only his crooked elbows which had caught in the gutter.

He managed to raise himself on the sheer strength of his forearms, leaning in at the same time on his stomach, and then he raised first his right knee and then the left — and at that moment a nervous spasm sparked through his tense body and a violent cramp crippled his legs.

He kept his head, remaining perfectly still until the

seizure passed; then he scrambled up onto the gutter. A few more leverings on the ladder and the inner end joggled past the obstacle and he was able to lower it all the way down to Balbi.

Casanova climbed through the window, lowered himself to the top rung and went shakily down to the floor.

The two fugitives explored the deep loft in pitch darkness. Casanova blundered upon a locked door and broke it open with the crowbar. Now they were in a small room which contained a key on a table — something like Alice's first adventure in Wonderland.

"Must be another door," Casanova said. They fumbled around in the dark and Balbi discovered the hidden door. The key worked, and they stepped into a corridor.

A little stone staircase led them down three stories to a room which the friar said was the chancery office. It was the best news in the world to Casanova, for it meant that they were definitely in St. Mark's and not in the Leads proper.

The door leading from the room had a complicated lock that could not be forced by the crowbar. Balbi began to wail that they would never find their way out of the dark labyrinth of rooms and corridors and locked doors, and Casanova savagely told him to close his mouth. He attacked one of the large upper wooden panels in the door with his tool.

Balbi was absolutely no help to him. He wrung his hands and whimpered that the splintering noise Casanova was making would bring all the jailers and inquisitors down on their heads.

In half an hour the hole was large enough but it was

rimmed with jagged shards of wood and it was five foot high. Balbi mounted a stool and Casanova shoved him through headfirst. Then he climbed up and started to wiggle through himself, Balbi tugging at his armpits from the other side. Casanova piled on top of the friar in a lump, his legs frightfully torn and bleeding.

Knowing that dawn was close at hand, they ran hastily down two flights of stairs and broke open a door leading to the main staircase, which took them to the office of the *Savio alla Scrittura*. There they were confronted by an enormous double door of the sort one would expect to find in a medieval castle.

Casanova took one look at this imposing obstacle and realized it would take a catapult to break it down or a train of gunpowder to blow it up. Bleakly he looked at his small crowbar and it seemed to say to him: *Hic fines possuit* — You have done with me; leave me to my fate.

But he didn't cast the faithful tool aside. It was the instrument of his freedom, and he treasured it. It was worthy to hang on the altar of release and liberty. Quite calmly he sat down and turned to the frantic friar.

"My part of the work is done," he said. "Now God or good fortune must do the rest. We cannot break through that door. Today is All Saints' Day and tomorrow the Day of the Dead, and quite possibly no one will think to come to the Palace during that time. But if anyone *does* come — the instant that door is opened I fly, and you must follow at my heels. More than that I can not offer."

The distraught friar went into a rage. "Madman!

Liar! Deceitful, treacherous wretch! You promised me freedom, and here you idly sit awaiting our hour of recapture!"

But he was wrong. Casanova had noticed a large built-in wardrobe on the far wall, and he was quickly on his feet and going through the aged finery he found hanging inside it. The unused clothing dated back to the last century and how it came to be in this place he could not imagine; but as his own clothes were now in dirty, bloody rags he donned a laced shirt, a brocade coat, velveteen pants and a plumed hat trimmed with Spanish goldpoint.

Then, out of mere idle curiosity, he opened a large barred window and looked into the street below. A number of early-morning pedestrians observed the odd out-of-date character standing in the window and wondered how such a person could be there at that time of day. Someone informed the keeper of the key.

Again the hand of fate. The doorkeeper, thinking someone must have been locked in the day before, arrived before the huge doors with a jangling keyring in his hand. Hearing the noise, Casanova sprang to the inside of the door with the crowbar ready to strike. Friar Balbi crowded against his back.

The great door swung open and the surprised doorkeeper gawked at the two fugitives. Taking advantage of the man's amazement Casanova wagged the crowbar jauntily as though it were a walking stick, said, "Thank you," and started walking down the steps, Friar Balbi following close behind.

Going at a good pace, but not giving the impression

of a man running away, Casanova went by the magnificent Giant's Staircase, trying to ignore Balbi's frantic hisses.

"Into the church! We can find sanctuary in the church!"

There was a time when hard-pressed criminals could seek immunity from arrest inside a church, but that period was long since passed. Friar Balbi in his terror had lost track of time. He was trying to clutch at straws that no longer existed.

"Be quiet, you fool!" Casanova whispered over his shoulder. "The age of sanctuary is gone. We must make our own."

Striding forcefully ahead in his last-century finery, with the harassed looking friar tight at his back, Casanova crossed the enormous courtyard and passed through the entrance of the Doges' Palace and, looking neither right nor left at the staring civilians, marched across the little square that led to the quay.

A gondola was just then tying up to the quay as Casanova and his trembling shadow tramped down the damp steps. Without a pause in his brisk stride Casanova stepped into the boat and called in a loud voice, "Take me to Fusina and fetch another man to help you," to the gondolier.

As the gondolier shouted for a boatman to come assist him, Casanova stepped into the draped midship compartment and sat himself on the cushions. The friar, cowed and trembling, hunkered at his side.

"We'll never reach Fusina!" he whispered. "The hue and cry will be after us any moment!"

The gondolier and his helper cast off and manned the stern oar, both of them peering curiously at the tawdrily dressed friar and the man garbed in the archaic finery. They took Casanova for a charlatan or an astrologer. The gondola wended around the corner of the custom house and into the canal of the Giudecca.

Casanova relaxed. He had no intention of going to Fusina. He had only called out that name in case some of the idlers on the quay later reported his destination to the police. A wise fox takes pains to throw the pursuing hounds off his track.

Halfway down the canal he called to the gondolier.

"Do you suppose we shall reach Mestre before nightfall?"

"But, signore, you bid me to go to Fusina."

"Fool!" Casanova cried. "I told you Mestre."

At this point the witless friar broke in to assure Casanova that the gondolier was right. "You definitely said Fusina," he stated. Casanova longed to give him a kick for his idiocy, but settled for a warning nudge in the friar's ribs. At the same time he burst into laughter.

"Well, I stand corrected. I must have given the wrong name by mistake. But the truth is, I want to go to Mestre."

"As you order, signore," the gondolier said. "I'll take you to England if you like."

"Bravo!" Casanova said. "Then go to Mestre with all haste."

Settling back on his cushions Casanova looked behind at the canal. It seemed to be more beautiful than he had ever seen it — mostly because no pursuing boats were coming after them. The morning was delicious, the air pure and the first sunbeams glorious upon the water. The gondola reached Mestre within an hour.

The year of Casanova's death is uncertain — somewhere between 1798 and 1803. For the sake of Trenck, Latude and Kermen, it is pleasing to note in Casanova's famous *Memoirs* that among the many personages he duped during his scandalous career, there appear the names of Frederick the Great and Madame de Pompadour.

CHAPTER 7

One Way Out

THE battle was over and the Spanish forces had pulled out to commence their retreat into Portugal, leaving the French victorious on the field. The quartermaster's men were now mopping up the spoils of war, collecting weapons and ammunition and picking up the wounded. The burial parties were wandering among the dead with their spades and canvas sacks, pilfering the pockets of every dead soldier before they buried his body.

Captain Hernan de Vargas raised his head cautiously over the lip of a shallow ravine and parted a whin bush to peer out at a corpse-littered meadow. French soldiers were there salvaging muskets. A spade clunked behind De Vargas and he turned apprehensively. A burial party was working in the opposite field, only fifty yards off. He slid back to the bottom of the ravine.

He was definitely cut off from the retreating Spaniards. He had been left behind on the battlefield among thousands of enemy soldiers!

It was 1809 and Napoleon's Peninsular War was nearly one year old. From all indications the war would probably drag on interminably, and De Vargas did not propose to rot in some French prison for years. He had

to find a way out, a means to escape from this accursed battlefield.

Obviously the first thing to do was to get out of the open ravine and into better cover. He started crawling toward a nearby scrub hill. Like all hills in Portugal it was gorse-clad and rocky, rising bluntly from between an undergrowth valley and an olive grove.

He skirted around the body of a French sergeant, and then around a Spanish major who had matched his head against a cannonball. A halo of flies had already gathered over the headless corpse. De Vargas shivered with disgust and crawled on hurriedly.

He stopped — frozen on all fours. There was a rustle

of movement in the olive grove up ahead. Someone, something was coming through the leaves toward the ravine!

He looked around for a weapon. There was nothing at hand; only a stock-smashed musket back by the dead sergeant. He reached for a rock . . .

A clump of heather trembled at the edge of the ravine and, slowly, a tousle-headed powder-stained face emerged and looked right to left fearfully. It was a Spanish artilleryman! De Vargas waved and the excited artilleryman slid into the ravine. The two Spaniards crawled to each other like long lost brothers.

"I am Private Pedro Bernardino, señor," the artilleryman whispered. "My battery was cut off when the French flanked our right wing. I have been crawling among the dead, seeking cover."

"We need a place to hide out the day," De Vargas said. "Perhaps tonight we can slip away under cover of the dark."

"I know the very place, señor, for I am a native of these parts. There is a cave in that hill yonder. Follow me."

It sounded ideal to De Vargas. He started crawling after Bernardino. Then an unhappy thought struck him.

"Suppose the French cut us off once we are in the cave? I don't want to place myself in a *cul-de-sac*."

"Impossible, señor! For I know of a way out. There is a small passage that leads directly through the hill and comes out into a tangle of hills beyond."

"Excellent, Bernardino! Then we will follow the passage into the hills and elude the French completely."

ONE WAY OUT

Bernardino hesitated; then murmured, *"Si señor."*

They came to another dead man and Bernardino paused to roll the body over to get at the soldier's haversack. De Vargas was shocked. "What are you doing? Only ghouls rob the dead!"

"We might need his rations, señor," Bernardino explained. "If we have to remain in the cave."

"But we don't intend to remain long in the cave. Besides, we both have our own rations, as well as a canteen of water each."

"Still —" Bernardino muttered, "better to be sure now than sorry later." He crawled on with the dead man's haversack. Frowning, De Vargas followed him.

The entrance to the cave was not what De Vargas had expected. In his mind he had been thinking it would be an upright cavernous opening. Instead, Bernardino pointed to a mere hole in the ground not much larger than the mouth of a cannon.

Now that they had reached their objective, Bernardino seemed suddenly hesitant. "After you, señor," he murmured, avoiding De Vargas' gaze. The captain eyed the hole doubtfully.

"Is it very deep?" he wondered.

"Uh — no señor, I do not believe so."

De Vargas, not at all reassured by Bernardino's uncertain answer, took the haversack and dropped it down the hole. He listened to it hit not too far below. He sat down and put his feet into the opening and started lowering himself into the pit.

The chute was very narrow — and longer than he

had anticipated. The rock funnel rose over his head and darkness swallowed him. He reached the limit of his upstretched arms and still his booted feet had not touched bottom. He stalled indecisively, not really wanting to drop into the mysterious black pit.

But it had to be done. Finally he let go.

Instantly his heels struck an abutment and he tipped forward and cracked his chin against rock, and then he plunged straight down and for a vivid second he thought he was shooting to his death in a deep pit.

His feet slammed on the bottom and he felt the jar in his back teeth. But he was all right, and he called to Bernardino.

"Is it safe, señor?"

"Of course, you fool. Come down!"

A moment later Bernardino came down in a sliding plunge, and De Vargas felt for him in the dark. "Why did you ask if it was safe? You said you had been here before."

"It was a long time ago, señor," Bernardino replied in a hedged tone. "When I was a mere boy."

A patch of light found its way in, and soon the eyes of the two fugitives became somewhat accustomed to the darkness. Bernardino started rummaging in his own haversack, coming up with a bit of candle and a tinder box. In a moment they had light and De Vargas looked around.

The cave was narrow and varied between five and six feet in height. The rocky walls were concave and slightly damp to the touch. He could not determine the length of the cavern.

"Where is the passage that leads through the hill?" he asked.

Bernardino was sitting on the ground going through the dead soldier's haversack. He did not look up when he answered.

"Uh — back there somewhere, señor," making a vague gesture toward the rear of the cave. "I don't think we should concern ourselves with it unless we have to. We are perfectly safe here. Tonight, when the French are gone, we will be able to slip away."

"But we could depart through the passage right now and escape into the hills beyond," De Vargas reasoned.

Bernardino was now eating the dead man's rations, and he mumbled through a mouthful of beef.

"The passage is a very hard route to follow, señor. Treacherous. We would do better not to use it unless we absolutely must."

Disgruntled, De Vargas gave in. He was not at all satisfied with Bernardino's evasiveness regarding the mysterious passage, but perhaps it *would* be wise to wait till nightfall. He sat down and made a short meal of hardtack, bully beef and canteen water — iron rations.

It was very still and quiet inside the belly of the hill, and the two Spaniards felt divorced from the upper world which had been turned into a slaughterhouse by Napoleon's boundless ambition. To conserve their scrap of candle they sat in the dark during the long afternoon. Then the glow of light from the cave's muzzle-like opening faded out and total blackness came over the two men. It was night.

They waited a full hour more, and then De Vargas

wedged himself into the chutelike tunnel and climbed up to the mouth. Even before he reached the rim his ears had detected the muted murmur of voices — French voices!

A campfire crackled only one hundred feet away, bathing the gorsy walls of the ravine a shocking orange, and a handful of French soldiers were lounging around the fire as they prepared their evening meal. The glow of other fires glittered along the upper reaches of the ravine. And suddenly a voice boomed over De Vargas' head.

"*Apportez-moi du thé, Henri!*"

De Vargas ducked back in a panic. The soldier who had called for tea was standing but two yards away! Sliding, dropping, losing cloth and skin on the rough protrusions, De Vargas tumbled into the cave. Bernardino grabbed at him in the dark, hissing frantically.

"*Valgame Dios, señor*, what is wrong?"

"Wrong?" De Vargas whispered furiously. "What is wrong is that we can't escape through the mouth of the cave. The French have set up a bivouac all along the ravine!"

To De Vargas' mind there was only one obvious course. They would have to take the passage through the cave — dangerous or not. He said so to Bernardino, but the artilleryman was now as evasive as a wily old trout at the sight of a baited fishhook.

"It would be far, far wiser to remain here, señor. The French will surely decamp with the dawn, for Napoleon's armies never hesitate to follow up their victories. Let us wait, señor, I pray you. Wait until the morrow."

ONE WAY OUT

So, grudgingly, De Vargas waited, curling up on the rocky floor to sleep. He was awake with the first scrap of light that filtered down from the upper world, and he started climbing up to it immediately. He inched his head over the rim for a peek into the dawn-filled ravine.

The French were at their morning cookfires. They showed no indications of speed in their speech or movements, and De Vargas was military-minded enough to read the familiar signs. The French had no intention of breaking camp that day. Hoping to prove himself wrong, he stayed at his post and observed the enemy for nearly two hours.

Nothing happened. The Frenchmen showed about as much aggressiveness as a hibernating bear. Greatly vexed, De Vargas slid into the cave to tell Bernardino the bad tidings.

"Perhaps they are planning a night march, señor," the nervous artilleryman suggested. "That must surely be the case."

"I tell you they are not! I wouldn't be surprised if they intended to make this a permanent reserve post. We will have to take the passage through the cave now, before our food and water run out. We are already down to one day's ration apiece."

"Let us wait only one day more, señor," Bernardino pleaded. "Then, if the French are not gone, we — uh — we shall see."

"No! I insist that we try your secret passage *now*. If you refuse to obey my order, then I shall take the passage by myself and leave you here alone!"

A sly note slipped into Bernardino's voice.

"That would be exceedingly foolhardy of you, my captain. Because without *me* to guide you, you would surely become lost in the cave. For the passage forks, you see. And unless I tell you which turn to take, you will undoubtedly perish in the attempt."

De Vargas saw the grim truth in this statement and realized that he was helpless. But he was not a man to sit idle when the gate of action stood open before him. For hours he tried to exhort the craven soldier to come over to his way of thinking; threatening, pleading, berating and reasoning with the adamant artilleryman. All to no avail. Bernardino refused to budge till the next day.

Night came and passed and dawn glimmered in the little hole above their heads. De Vargas made his third ascent up to the rim. Again the same static scene: the Frenchmen leisurely fooling with their cookfires, as if breaking camp and marching on were the last item on their warlike agenda.

De Vargas observed them till mid-morning; then, making a grim resolution, he climbed down into the cave.

"They are still there," he informed the artilleryman, "and they show every indication of remaining there for some time. We will now take your secret passage. We *must* take it, for our food and water will not last another day."

Bernardino said nothing. He wrung his hands in mute despair and refused to meet De Vargas' searching gaze.

"It is dangerous," he finally murmured. "Very very

dangerous. We might become lost in the bowels of the hill."

"But you told me the passage leads directly through the hill," De Vargas argued. "You said you knew the way."

Bernardino was strangely silent — and it was only then that De Vargas fully understood the breed of man with which fate had elected to cloister him. He let out his breath heavily.

"You don't know the way, eh Bernardino?" he accused his companion. "You have been lying from the very beginning. You haven't even ever been in this cave! Is that correct?"

Bernardino hung his head like a shamed cur.

"Forgive me, my captain," he whined. "I only meant the best. I knew of the cave because my grandfather showed me the entrance to it when I was a boy. It was he who explored this place in his youth."

"Very well. At least we have *something* to go on. Did he tell you about the passage leading through the hill?"

"*Si, si, señor!*" Bernardino was insistent on that point. "He told me he had explored the passage to its exit in the hills beyond. But he also told me of its dangers!"

"Never mind its dangers! What instructions did he give you?"

"To stay always to the right, señor. 'The right way is to the right' were his very words!"

"*Bueno!*" De Vargas cried. "Light the candle — and we'll try the right way."

There was a small hole in the back wall of the cave

and, to De Vargas' harassed mind, it had the foul aspect of a rathole. Nevertheless he took the candle and got down on all fours and crawled into it. Bernardino had no option but to follow him. To remain behind meant either starvation or capture.

The tunnel was short but it forked at a wide spot. De Vargas bore to the right, and within a minute he found that the roof of the cave rose and he could stand up. Bernardino, trembling violently, crowded against his back.

The tunnel was now high and broad and the two Spaniards strode forward as if they were walking down a corridor inside a mighty fortress.

This spaciousness lasted for some one hundred yards; then the ceiling began to lower and, if they were not careful, they brushed the roof with their heads, and tiny particles of crystal-like rock rained down on them.

Abruptly the floor of the tunnel turned to a stinking mud and patches of stagnant water glittered evilly in the candlelight. The rock-ribbed walls literally oozed an inky moisture.

The roof lowered — lowered — and now they were bending over and going forward in a humped posture; next they were on hands and knees; and finally they were flat on their stomachs, worming doggedly through the shallow pools and the malodorous slime, with the cold muck soaking through their clothes and coating their hides.

"Better than a French prison, eh Bernardino?" De Vargas called back, hoping to encourage both of them.

"Not much, señor!" Bernardino responded unhappily.

De Vargas snaked on for a few feet. The ceiling pressed down so low that he was flattened in the mushy mud and it was all he could do to concentrate half of his mind on keeping the fluttering candle out of the wet. He did not care to think what it would be like to find himself in such a fix without a light.

The eighteen-inch-high passage curved gradually to the right and he followed it. Forcing his head and shoulders around the tight bend — his body squeezing the soft mud aside and the rock roof and floor pressing him from above and below — he wormed ahead through four yards of this vise-like passage. All at once he discovered that he could no longer bring his crooked elbows alongside his chest to give his prone body leverage.

The narrow, circular tunnel was now touching his rib cage on either side. He glanced ahead at the little peak of flame trembling spasmodically at the tip of the muddy candle clutched in his right fist.

If it goes out, he thought bleakly, *I'll go mad.*

He inched forward for another three feet, feeling like the Biblical camel that could not squeeze through the Needle's Eye. Then — miraculously — the crawl hole widened, the ceiling sloped upward and the two fugitives found themselves standing hunched over in a low, broad cavern.

Bernardino looked like a man made of mud in the wan candlelight. Only the whites of his eyes and the gleam of his teeth signified a frightened human being.

"Enough, señor!" he proclaimed in a chattering voice. "I cannot go through such an ordeal again! It is more than the brain can endure!"

De Vargas was ready to agree with him; yet according to his doubtful calculations they were now in the very heart of the hill. In short — at the point of no return, where it would be just as futile to go back as to try to go ahead. Only one thing was certain: they could not remain static in the damp crowded cavern where they were now crouching.

"Do as you wish," he said tersely. "If you decide to remain in this stinking chamber till you starve, that is your business. I am going on."

Suiting the action to his words he set off toward the rear of the cavern. When he looked back he discovered the mud-daubed apparition of the artilleryman close behind him.

The subterranean chamber graduated into a smooth, steep rock slope which angled upward. Scrabbling like a beetle on an uptilted pane of glass, De Vargas managed to reach a small pear-shaped vault in the ceiling.

An old stump of candle was in a niche in the wall; possibly left by Bernardino's grandfather a generation ago. De Vargas tried to light it but the aged and damp wick would not burn. The air was definitely bad, he suddenly realized. The little tent of flame on his candle was starting to leap in short sharp flares.

He rubbed at his moist face. His brain was going limp and his thoughts were sloshing around as if he had been drinking a heady wine.

Must keep moving . . . must keep to the right . . . the right way is to the right . . .

A trickle of moisture dribbled down the face of the rock wall in front of him, coming from still another rathole-like opening. *Good,* he thought dizzily. *Stay to the right.* He crouched and pushed into the hole, holding the wretched light of the dying candle before him.

The tunnel forked and he called back to Bernardino as he started to crawl.

"This way, comrade. It can't be much farther!"

He wedged himself into the aperture, into the oozy mud and trickling water. Bernardino, now nearly witless with fear and despair, followed him with his face only inches behind De Vargas' feet. Slowly, foot by foot, they shoved their way forward with the mighty mass of the entire hill pressing in on their constricted bodies.

Again the tunnel narrowed and De Vargas was barely able to squirm ahead. His strength began to flag. A bubbling sweat broke from his pores. The mud became mushier. The candle flame faltered. The rock ceiling pressed down on his head, on his humped shoulders. He was inching along with his head to one side, his left cheek sliding through the cold wet mud which clogged his ear and overflowed into his mouth . . .

His outstretched hands banged into rock. Dead halt.

Angling his gaze around he saw a small rock ridge directly across his path, like a wrinkle of stone. He wiggled himself a little farther on and managed to get his outthrust arms over the barrier but not his head. There wasn't enough clearance.

"I can't go on," he called back to Bernardino.

"You must, señor!" Bernardino's muffled voice hissed at his heels. "It is the only way."

Gasping for breath, straining every muscle in his

tightly drawn body, De Vargas squirmed against the rock in a Herculean effort to force his head sideways over the ridge. It simply would not fit. The human skull will not compress a fraction of an inch.

With millions of tons of earth pressing down on him, his heaving chest caught in a merciless squeeze, he knew he was truly in a hopeless *cul-de-sac*.

"Go back, Bernardino!"

"I cannot, señor! There was barely room to squirm forward! How can I possibly squirm *backward*?"

The candle flared brilliantly and snuffed out and a great silent wave of blackness covered the two prone men. De Vargas groaned. Bernardino's head pushed demandingly against his heels. The immense weight of the ponderous hill pressed on his sweating back . . .

He went a little wild. He tried to shove up, to raise the entire mighty hill with his back. In response the tunnel seemed to close in on him from all four sides like a great clenched fist. He couldn't breathe, couldn't think. He only knew he had to get out!

Couldn't go ahead, couldn't raise up, couldn't turn to either side, and Bernardino was holding him from going back — was, in fact, trying to force him to go on!

The air was so foul it was like warm soup and his ribs were aching in the viselike squeeze and he couldn't keep his face out of that stinking oozy mud and the tons of rock were crushing him. He felt like a damp seed buried deep in the warm blind earth.

"Go back, Bernardino!" he cried.

Bernardino was now in a wild panic himself. He

wailed and whimpered and banged the top of his head against De Vargas' heels as if he meant to hammer the captain through the hole.

"Go back!" De Vargas shouted.

"I cannot! I cannot! I cannot!" Bernardino was yelling and bumping blindly at De Vargas' heels and making weird animal noises in his throat.

De Vargas sucked at the bad air and kicked at Bernardino's head with his right foot — kicked again and again, viciously and desperately, his fogged brain crying, *Out out out!*

Strangely, the blows seemed to stabilize Bernardino's senses. He started to squirm himself backward through the tight crawl hole, still whimpering like a wounded cur.

De Vargas followed him, painfully, slowly, one small back-shoving movement at a time, like a drowsy inchworm traveling in reverse. Suddenly the tunnel expanded in height and breadth and he paused to feel around in the pitchy dark. His brain was still swimming sluggishly from the foul air and he couldn't seem to think straight.

Keep to the right, always to the right . . .

A faint wisp of a draft touched his mud-dripping body and he had enough presence of mind left to realize they were in better air.

"The tinder box, Bernardino. Quickly!"

Bernardino was in a mental funk. He was still trying to shove himself backward on his stomach in the mud. De Vargas found him in the dark, took the tinder box, struck a spark and got the sputtery candle going. In its weird jellylike glow he saw two small openings side by side. The crawlhole on the left was the one from which they had just backed out.

He had led the way into the wrong hole! No wonder they had been trapped. He started to laugh crazily in relief and excitement.

"This way, Bernardino! This way!"

He leveled himself in the mud and crawled forward. Bernardino followed him like a dazed man, whimpering pitifully.

Again the ceiling lowered and the rock walls closed in, and the air became thick and heavy and the candle fluttered and faltered. De Vargas squirmed and inched through the ghastly mud. Something was wrong. He could barely force himself along.

Then he saw a ripple of rock across his path. His groggy brain had sent him directly back into the left-hand passage! He nearly broke down and cried with frustration.

"Go back, Bernardino!"

Again they made the long slow painful passage back to the fork in the tunnel. By this time Bernardino was practically a gibbering idiot. De Vargas patted him reassuringly on the back.

"I will get us out now, amigo. Only a little more courage."

He crawled into the right-hand tunnel and Bernardino followed him mechanically. It was bad at first but it gradually became better. The ceiling raised, the walls widened and wisps of fresher air stirred along the passage.

Their stump of candle, however, was nearly down to a mere bit of charred wick in De Vargas' burnt fingers. It died an abrupt death. But just as Bernardino gave a groan of despair, De Vargas gave a shout of triumph that resounded thunderously along the black corridor.

A tiny glimmer of light shone in the darkness ahead.

Minutes later the two mud-coated exhausted men climbed out through a vertical crack in the granite wall and found themselves standing on a gorsy shoulder overlooking a tortuous valley winding its way through a tangle of lonely hills.

It was like a wonderland of freedom.

Hernan de Vargas' story is based more on legend than printed fact. I have not been able to verify it but I believe it is true as told.

CHAPTER 8

The Man from Devil's Island

THE solitary confinement cell-block on Ile St. Joseph had no roof. It exposed all of its small cells to the merciless equator heat and to the sudden and overwhelming tropical rains. No one seemed to care how the prisoners suffered from this brutal arrangement.

Each cell was six-by-six, with an iron door and six iron bars over the top. A central corridor ran between the cells, and this passageway was roofed with a narrow catwalk which allowed the pacing guards to look into the cells below.

St. Joseph was one of the three islands of the Iles du Salut, which were thirty miles from the main penal camp at Cayenne on French Guiana. The other two islands were Royale and Ile du Diable — Devil's Island. Diable was the smallest of the three and it had given the entire penal colony its infamous name, though actually it had never housed more than a handful of political prisoners at a time. It was a picnic spot compared to life on Joseph or Royale or any of the many mainland camps.

St. Joseph was used to confine the incorrigible prisoners who were transferred from the mainland. The word "incorrigible" usually had reference to the stubborn convicts who were determined to escape from Guiana at any cost.

Such a man was the French convict Dieudonné. He had been arrested by the Paris police in 1912 as a member of the famous Bonnot gang. Protesting his innocence had done him no good. He had been condemned to death with the rest of the gang. One by one the bandits had gone to the guillotine. It was Dieudonné's turn next.

Then, at the last moment, Bonnot himself had made a deathbed statement that Dieudonné had not taken part in the gang's crimes. The French authorities did not relish admitting they had arrested and condemned an innocent man; besides, they only had the word of Bonnot, a thief, that Dieudonné was not a criminal. So, to resolve the matter (also to hush it up) they commuted his sentence to forced labor in Guiana, for life.

He was twenty-eight when he reached Cayenne, and he was still avowing his innocence. The penal authorities put him to work in one of the boiling Guiana swamps, manhandling the enormous wacapou logs. Convicts died like flies out there in the steaming morass, but Dieudonné was determined to survive; more than that — to escape.

He made his first break through Dutch Guiana to Paramaribo, but was arrested on board a ship bound for Java. The following year he stole a boat and got away with seven other convicts. The French mail ship caught them off Demerara. He was given four years of solitary confinement on St. Joseph for that attempt.

Returned to the mainland, he ran away from Nouveau Camp and made for the sea again. Unluckily his boat ran aground and he was captured for the third time. Undaunted, he sawed his way out of his cell, stole a boat and put to sea. The boat leaked and had no rudder; and he had made a sail out of an old shirt and a pair of pants. Five days later, off Marowana in British Guiana, the boat capsized and he was rescued and returned to Cayenne.

He next made a double escape — first, from the invalid camp at Cayenne, second, from the St. Laurent prison. Apprehended almost immediately, he was sent back to the cell block on St. Joseph — with a sentence of ten years' solitary confinement.

The year was 1927. He had served over fourteen years of penal punishment in Guiana. For fourteen years he had been gambling his life against his liberty, and he was now more determined than ever to win his freedom.

He would do the impossible, what had never been accomplished before: he would escape from St. Joseph. It would be the greatest escape in Devil's Island history.

Everything was against him: the watchful guards, the iron-barred and concrete-walled cell, even his own health. After fourteen years in the Guiana inferno he was emaciated and suffered from violent bouts of prison fever. And even if he could break out of his cell, there was still twenty miles of sea between the island and the nearest point of the mainland.

And everyone knew that the sharks, *not the human guards,* were the real watchdogs of Devil's Island. The shark-infested waters around the Iles du Salut (meaning Islands of Health!) had a long and fearsome reputation. They were the watery disposal units of the penal colony.

But all that must wait until he was free from his cell; free from the six overhead bars and the six feet square of concrete.

Like a cooped cat unable to remain still, he started pacing his cell, thinking. Twice up, twice back. Two paces up, two paces back, grazing the flaking walls as he turned, brushing his board pallet and slop bucket, again the walls, step, step, turn . . .

The sun was high and the heat was heavy and awful as it gathered and concentrated to press down upon the men exposed in the cells below. Sweat bubbled from his skin as heat that was almost fluid in its weight and closeness converged upon his body from all sides — from the walls and floor of his cell, from the burning iron bars above.

He stared up at the six bars covering his cell, and listened to the rhythmical beat of the pacing guard going back and forth across the elevated catwalk. He counted the paces; ninety-one down, turn, ninety-one back — and the khaki-clad legs of the guard flickered across Dieudonné's overhead bars.

So — he could count on 182 paces from the time the

guard passed over his cell and returned. Just about 180 seconds, or three minutes.

The guard clomped over his cell. Dieudonné sprang for the bars above, did a chin-up and looped one hand and arm between two bars, hanging now by one forearm. His free hand explored the end of the corner bar.

The overhead bars were two inches thick, made of iron, their ends bedded deep in concrete. But through decades of tropic rains and terrific heat the concrete had softened and cracked. Not a lot, just a little, but . . .

He dropped into his cell and raised a hand to his mouth. Laughter that verged on hysteria bubbled up through his lips. It might well take a long time — but he was going to break out of his cell by way of the catwalk!

Everyday now, and night too, Dieudonné sprang up to the bars — three minutes at a time, counting the seconds in his mind. Hanging by his right arm on the corner bar he worked feverishly on the second bar from the end, steadily shaking and wrenching and levering it loose, watching the little specks of loosened concrete glance down the wall of his cell.

He rolled the motes of concrete dust into small spitballs and embedded them in his slop bucket. The guards seldom entered his cell, but he was taking no chances.

The measured clomp of boots, the creak of leather and the rustle of starched khaki always warned him of a guard's approach; and he was always ready for their survey — standing in a stooped position in his cell, his hands behind his back, contemplating the floor. The perfect picture of idle and abject despair!

When the sun began its diurnal descent and the heat of the day slackened slightly with the faint land breeze that blew off the mainland jungle, hobnailed boots clunked in the corridor and there came the sour smell of lukewarm onion soup. The soup was passed in to each convict through an aperture in the cell doors; at the same time the prisoners passed out their slop buckets.

This procedure continued for seven months. It took Dieudonné that long to wrench loose the second bar. Then he started to work on the corner bar.

Three times he was nearly spotted by one of the guards. He had to be very careful. Convicts frequently went mad in the solitary cells and many of the half-demented men would leap up and hang from their bars like so many caged apes, gibbering and cursing. It was called "crawling the iron" and it warranted brutal punishment if noticed by the guards.

The corner bar was easier. In three months' time he detected that it had a little play to it. He continued his sporadic labor, wrenching, pulling, heaving, the powdered cement falling upon his head and shoulders in a fine, soft rain.

Day in, day out, baking by day, sweltering by night; and always there was Roussenq, the mad poet, with his daily howling babble. Sometimes when Roussenq's yelling would mount higher and higher, the guards sluiced him with cold water. Dieudonné did not want to become like that.

Another month passed . . .

Down the sky darkness fell, slaking a little the heat that had lain upon the land and the windless sea. Silence

— only darkness now, outside and inside the cell block. Darkness relieved temporarily by sheet lightning far north, born in the storm-breeding mountains of Guiana. But no thunder rumbles were audible on St. Joseph, and when the distant lightning died out the darkness was redoubled. Then a hard black-crystal rain swept in and began drumming violently on the tin roofs of the camp.

Dieudonné sprang for the bars. This was the perfect night for escape. He went to work urgently on the corner bar. The rain hammered down on his head and face. His bent forearm was numb from fingertips to elbow; from elbow to shoulder it sparkled with pain. His suspended body cramped and recramped.

Outside, unmuffled by the thick walls, sounded the harsh drumbeats of the driving rain on the roofs; beats which seemed to conflict like several stations all sending at once on the same wave. After a while the roof on the administration building drummed furiously as if telling the others to shut up and listen and then take their turns. But the outer medley still went on, though softer now. Then it ceased. The rain had stopped.

And at that moment the end of the corner bar was free in Dieudonné's hand.

Clomp — clomp — boots coming along the catwalk. Dieudonné dropped into his cell, threw himself on his pallet, pretending sleep. A guard paused overhead, casting the crystalline glare of his flashlight through the bars.

The light winked out, the guard moved off, and Dieudonné stood up. The muscles tightened in his calves and thighs. He leaped at the bars overhead, thrusting himself up against them. The time was now!

"*Pardieu!*" the guard cried. He had not gone five paces away!

Some final mental barrier gave way within Dieudonné. He yelled like a prehistoric man trapped by the primordial mysteries that were too much for his elemental comprehension. He shoved up terrifically at the two loosened bars. One came loose in his hand, and he rammed and shouldered his body between the other bar and the wall, his threshing feet pawing at the cell door, and then he was up and out and scrabbling over the edge of the catwalk.

The guard was rushing him, pawing at his holstered pistol. Dieudonné swung the iron bar, clipped the man alongside the head and caught him as he started to drop. He took the guard's pistol and pocketknife; then lowered the limp man into his cell and replaced the two bars.

He took off along the wet catwalk, raced into the breeze until he reached the end of the walk. He went bounding down the free stairs at the corner of the cell block — didn't wait for the last five steps but took them in a wild leap and hit running. The moon was creeping out as he charged across the deserted compound and went over the stockade wall.

He had successfully taken the first giant step.

Now he was in the jungle. Heavy trees, moist with the night rain, wrapped with vines, interlaced by bush cord, intermingled with thorn thickets, formed a matted mass almost impenetrable. But not for a man nearly out of his mind with fear, fever and determination.

Dieudonné slipped through the maze like a fleeing

wraith, leaping an occasional bush with elasticity, veering around stout trunks, sliding between others, holding an erratic course which gradually bore to the sea.

Abruptly the jungle opened like a tawdry stage curtain and he stumbled onto the rocky shore. Sodden with sweat, clothes and skin ripped and daubed red, his face bruised and dirty, he went to work with the knife, chopping down banana stems. Quickly he bound together a bunch of them with bush cord, like an ungainly bundle of sticks, and lugged his banana raft into the shallow surf.

It was the most haphazard raft imaginable, but it was all he had with which to breast the great coastal rollers of the Atlantic — that, and his courage. It takes a *man* to try to escape from the Iles du Salut. But then all the Guiana convicts were agreed that Dieudonné was a man, and when *they* said that a man was a man, they meant that he was strong, reckless, defiant, of indomitable spirit, and that he would never give up the struggle for liberty.

He was only able to place the upper half of his body on the flimsy, soggy raft. His legs dragged behind in the water and he kicked with his feet. He held the pistol out of the water as much as possible. The stars appeared like illuminated paint-drops spattered on a vast blackboard. He looked up at the panorama of tropical night as he hitch-kicked and rocked with the moving surface.

He was drifting now in the endless splendor of sea and night, but under him lay eternity. And it came to him that there was treasure, human treasure buried in the depths of night and he was guiding one tiny bit of its precious cargo through a world that recognized only two elements — liquid and air. They were unconscious of him, unconcerned over his doubtful existence. He was but a bit of vitalized matter, an insignificant speck of flotsam, and yet he was holding his own between them.

He felt like laughing. He was a little unbalanced.

Then something brushed against his knee, cold and slick. He recoiled violently from the living contact, twisting and kicking viciously at the water. Shark? Barracuda? An elongated streak darted beneath his little raft. He turned quickly, looking, and tried to pull himself up onto the raft.

Without warning he was caught in a bayonet charge of dense silver. A great school of pikelike fish with long pointed jaws filled with needle teeth swarmed past his flanks. Barracuda!

He hunched himself, feeling completely naked and vulnerable. The school swished by and he pawed at his face with a dripping hand. He pictured them tearing into his defenseless body with their mouths of solid teeth. Not a pretty thought. He kicked on.

Something was wrong. Ripples of white-lipped water formed on his right and expanded. From the dark distance he heard a violent splashing. Something darted before his face, smacked hard against the surface and disappeared. Then there was a roiling in the water.

It was feeding time at sea!

Millions of tiny fires burst into being. Phosphorescence purled the water a skim-milk white. He was adrift in the middle of a fairyland of terror. Flying fish skittered across the choppy black surface and fat-bodied hunters streaked after them. Boneless slimy things twisted and churned silently through the sea.

Dieudonné changed his course, trying to work his way out of the writhing arena. It was impossible. Wherever he turned the chase thrashed on. Suddenly a great square block reared before him like a house caught in a cataclysmic upheaval, blacking out the dark sky. Water drained from its shimmering sides and splattered.

Dieudonné switch-backed with his legs, trying to retreat. For a long moment the thing hung poised above him — then it dropped flat and slammed the sea. The backwash crashed over him. Something scraped against his thigh and, turning, he fired at the black water with the pistol.

Get me out of this mess, he prayed. *Get me out!*

Perhaps it was the slam of the giant manta ray or the crack of the pistol that chased the smaller creatures away. He didn't know; but abruptly the sea settled into its infinite silence and he kicked slowly along, trembling from cold and nerves.

It was almost dawn when the first shark caught up to him.

He watched it knife through the gloom like a futuristic submarine. It was a seven-foot whitetip, perfectly balanced and controlled by its heterocercal tail. Dieudonné opened fire with the pistol and the startled shark flicked its tail, jackknifed and fled underwater.

Dieudonné saw the sea. It rolled away from him in the glassy dawn, and the towering, ragged majesty of

Guiana hulked before him. It waited, sweltering and brooding beneath a saffron sky, the fronds and heads of palms resting unmoved under the constant swoops and descents of vultures.

He grinned and began the last long leg for shore. He had taken the second giant step.

Time was vitally precious. By now the unconscious guard had surely been discovered and the alarm was out; and Dieudonné had a long hard road to go. He intended to make his way southeast through the jungle to Brazil. The wet, slimy, treacherous, friendly jungle. Full of danger and fever, it was more friendly than man or the sea.

The bad part about a jungle escape, as every convict knew, was the half-savage native trackers. The penal authorities paid the Guiana Indians a good price for the capture of all runaway prisoners. And those dusky men of the wilderness knew their business.

But so did Dieudonné. He had had fourteen years in which to study the deceptive mysteries of Guiana jungles. If he could cross the Camopi River, he was certain he could shake his pursuers.

He trotted down a trail. He knew where, a couple of miles on, a tapir trail crossed it. He would take that; and then, judging by its direction and the local topography, he hoped it would come out at another trail he knew that led south. The jungle swallowed him.

Up in the high treetops were monkeys and parrots playing in the sun, though Dieudonné saw it only in diamondlike glimpses. Eternal shade lay on the jungle floor, a dim green light that filtered through the dense mat of vines — lush, creeping, thorny trailers that caught at his feet.

Three cartridges left in his pistol; not much to supply him with food for the seven days he estimated it would take him to reach the Camopi. His first shot bagged a gaudy macaw. Rather a meager return for a precious bullet. He attacked the leathery fowl with a voracious appetite, saving half of it for the next day.

He tried to maintain a pace of twenty miles a day — not an easy task in that writhing jungle where any kind of danger might be lurking around the next tree. He spent the nights in the high crotches of trees where neither mosquitoes nor jaguars could reach him, making a sort of orangutan roost of liana vines.

The seven days passed and he still had not sighted the Camopi. Food was the relentless question now — his staying power; the sheer necessity of nourishment for human strength and endurance. His cartridges were gone and he had eaten nothing in forty-eight hours. Now it was the evening of the eighth day and he wondered if he could risk the time to stop and make a game trap.

He couldn't. There was a sudden lurid flicker of lights far back in the damp foliage. The Guiana Indians were after him!

The night was a running agony of demoniac vines that snatched at his scrambling feet, of thorny trailers rasping across his face. And always, behind him, were the confident voices of the savages as they picked up his dodging trail again and again. He managed to keep ahead till daylight, but he was slowing up.

He was still covering ground, still grimly ahead, his face haggard and his lids drooping over bloodshot eyes. But there was a spark of the ultimate desperation in his eyes. He was preparing himself to risk everything on a final gamble.

As he ran he slashed a palm sapling with his knife and whittled it into a barbed spear such as the Indians used. There was no hesitation in his mind. Either the trick would work and he would be free, or it would fail and he would be hauled back to solitary confinement — this time, perhaps, for life.

The jungle floor sloped. A depression always meant a swamp, a still oozing place where scaly things squirmed. The main pool was some 100 yards in width and like all Guiana swamps it contained its own special brand of chill horror.

Dieudonné had seen the cold-eyed menace that lurked in those warm, slimy pools. Electric eels — mottled gray and leprous white; thick as a man's arm, stubby and powerful, capable of stunning a horse. They would glide smoothly under a wading man's legs, flick up head and tail to contact, and discharge a shock that stiffened the wretched victim rigid.

He paused at the edge of the pool, studying the scummy water. Suddenly he plunged the spear into the shallows and snatched it ashore. A four-foot muscular eel was writhing powerfully on the barbed stick. Its vicious, crazed eyes watched the man balefully as it wriggled and its gash of a mouth filled with innumerable tiny teeth snapped at the spear.

Dieudonné cut off its head with his knife, sliced the

body open and drew out the liver and roe sack. They were filled with a fishy smelling oil and he rubbed it into his skin and clothes. Then, hesitantly, he started wading into the stagnant pool. The voices of his pursuers were very close behind.

At each step he wondered if he would suddenly feel a fat, slimy thing snuggle up to his body, if there would be the paralyzing shock that would render him helpless, if he would sink and drown. And if then, later, when he was putrid and decomposed, the gruesome creatures in the muck would eat him.

He took another step, another — something touched his right leg but there was no devastating shock. Maybe he was going to be lucky; maybe he could trick the hideous eels into accepting him for one of their own kind. That was the theory of the eel oil.

Maybe . . .

He stepped into a submerged pit and floundered for a wild moment up to his chin. Nothing happened. No nerve-numbing jolt stretched him out. He found firmer footing and the green-scum water dropped to his chest. He waded on, deeper and deeper into the liquid mire.

Thirty feet to go . . . twenty . . . the mushy bottom was rising under his feet . . . then a sudden piercing exclamation behind him. He glanced back, catching his breath.

Four Guiana savages, armed with spears and blowguns, stood on the distant bank. One of them blew a dart at him through his gun but the distance was too great for accuracy.

Wringing wet and adrape with clinging water weeds

and foul muck, Dieudonné waded out on the opposite shore. He squelched up the bank to the green wall of the jungle and turned to send a derisive laugh back at his balked pursuers.

The four savages were lined along the bank contemplating the opaque water. They had seen Dieudonné wade the pool and emerge unscathed, and they could not know that he had first greased himself with eel oil.

They talked it over hastily. Obviously the pool was not deep; there were no caymans or eels, and so it must be comparatively safe. Besides, if they wasted time in building a raft or in catching eels to rub themselves with oil, their prey would escape them. The Camopi was very close, and beyond that was Brazil.

They came to a decision and started wading into the pool.

Dieudonné ducked behind a chunto palm to observe their progress through the lacy fronds. They were using their spears as poles as they waded farther and farther into the morass. They were mighty wary at first; then, as they proceeded unharmed, they began to grin and call encouragements to one another.

Watching them come on, foot by foot, Dieudonné had a dread thought. What if those deadly eels were vicious only at certain seasons of the year? What if they didn't attack the savages after all? Any obscure law of nature might control them. Meanwhile he had let priceless time slip by.

He started to turn, to run again — but paused, staring back at the money-greedy Indians who were now plunging eagerly onward.

All at once the native on the far left cried and jumped frenziedly high out of the water, then fell back shrieking, his legs paralyzed, flailing at the water with his hands.

The man next to him, wading waist deep, turned with a look of horror as a thick, livid, muscular thing zigzagged toward him and nuzzled up to his hip to make a contact that would send a galvanic current through his nerve center.

The man's shriek ripped through the brooding swamp like a buzz saw going through hard pine. His body jerked backward, bending like a drawn bow, and he sank in a welter of bubbles, twitching spastically.

The third man, chest high, threw up both his hands, dropping his useless blowgun, and clutched helplessly at the empty air. One of the squirming eels had caught him square in the spine and he couldn't even force out a scream. He toppled forward into a green blanket of floating scum and went under with all four limbs rigid.

The fourth man, realizing that they had floundered into a nest of the ghastly things, spun about and started thrashing his way back through the awesome ooze.

He never made it. Beyond him in that terrifying water, fearsome shapes lay huddled, half submerged under green slime. These were the dreaded caymans — the tropical crocodiles that infest the South American swamps and rivers.

Spellbound, Dieudonné watched the last man disappear screaming under the green-scum surface. Then he was standing all alone on the spongy bank. He shook his head and turned away — south, for the Camopi and Brazil.

In July of that same year, 1927, Dieudonné was arrested in Brazil. But France, by this time, was ready to admit its mistake. He was granted a full pardon by the French government and was returned to his native land a free citizen.

He was forty-three and he had been in Guiana fifteen years — for a crime he had not committed.

One last and ironic note on Dieudonné. His name, in French, means *God-given*.

CHAPTER 9

To Hang It on a Limb

THE judge looked down at the short, slight young man standing before him and said, "Robert Burns, I sentence you to from six to ten years at hard labor on the chain gang."

Robert Elliot Burns was a young, penniless hobo adrift in the Deep South in April 1922. Having no friends, he made the mistake of falling in with two other drifters, and told them he was looking for a job. They said they could get him one and they took him to a nearby grocery store. Then they told him he would have to help them hold up the store.

Burns refused and started to walk away. One of the tramps shoved a pistol in his ribs and threatened to shoot him if he tried to get out of it. Burns saw he had no option and agreed.

The store was held up and the tramps took $5.80 from the till. Twenty minutes later all three men were arrested. Burns was tried and sentenced for a crime he had had no intention whatever of committing. Four days later he was on his way to an isolated chain gang in the tupelo-clad hills.

The camp was a stockade on a level red-dust esplanade, blazing under a fiery Southern sun. Burns was handed a cotton suit of "stripes" — no underwear or socks — and a pair of broken brogans four sizes too big. Then he was taken to the blacksmith's shed.

A steel shackle was riveted on each ankle, joined by a heavy iron chain. This was the strad chain and it had thirteen links, which made it impossible for a man to take a full step. An upright chain was connected to the middle of the strad. The upright was three feet long and had an iron ring on its free end, which looped to the back of a convict's belt.

Burns was then escorted to the barracks, or bullpen. It was a long wooden building, heavily barred, with cots and mattresses along each side and open toilets in the center aisle. The greasy mess-hall was at the far end.

Lights were out at 8:30 every night. A long bull chain was run down alongside the foot of each cot and each prisoner had to feed the bull chain through the iron ring on his upright chain. The bull chain was then padlocked at both ends of the building.

If a man had to get up in the night he could move only three feet away from his cot. But first he had to call "Getting up" and wait for the guard's reply "Get up." The heavy clanking of his chains would then disturb all the other sleeping prisoners.

The chains the convicts wore weighed twenty pounds and were a permanent part of them. They worked in them and slept in them. They could only be cut off with a hammer and cold chisel.

At 3:30 A.M. a guard would draw the bull chain

through the upright rings, and if a convict did not wake up to hold his ring steady he would be yanked out of bed and dragged by his feet to his neighbor's cot.

The convicts were herded into the mess hall and ate by lamplight. Breakfast was a cup of stale coffee, a chunk of fried dough made of grease and flour, and a dab of fried pork. It was so bad that Burns couldn't get his down on his first morning.

Prisoners were assembled in the yard at 4:15 and a squad chain united them into gangs of twenty. Then they scrambled on to trucks — two guards per vehicle, each armed with pistol and automatic shotgun. The trucks rolled into the predawn dark, carrying their suffering cargo of humanity.

The chain gangs worked on roads and in swamps. The heat was sweltering, the dust stifling, and the brutal guards bullyragged them continuously to "keep the lick." On the shovel, the speed of the lick was sixteen shovelfuls a minute or 960 shovelfuls an hour — in twenty pounds of constricting chains, in the blazing sun, thirteen hours a day, six days a week!

Six to ten years of this inhuman torture? Burns' brain reeled.

No one was allowed a moment's rest. If a convict wanted to wipe the sweat from his brow he had to call "Wiping it off" and wait until the guard replied "Wipe it off." Each man received a cup of tepid water to drink once an hour — usually.

At noon a guard would call "Lay 'em down," and the weary convicts would lay down their tools to eat. The food was served from a galvanized iron bucket and it consisted of corn pone and red beans, unpalatable and full of sand and worms.

Lunch over, Burns was put on a pick gang. They worked in mechanical unison and kept at it in rhythmical cadence, the tempo of the lick regulated by a chanting Negro.

"Raise 'em high!" the Negro sang.

"*Ump!*" grunted the gang and all the picks went up.

"And bring 'em down!"

"*Ahh!*" and all the picks came down — over and over again all through the torrid day, until sunset.

Chained to the truck again they were driven back to camp, where they hobbled painfully into the barracks in single file. A burly guard stood at the doorway and inspected their chains, calling, "Come by me . . . come by me . . . come by me."

There were three tin basins of water for 100 dirty, sweat-drenched convicts. No towels or soap. Filing into the mess hall they received their supper — corn pone, fried pig fat and a dose of sorghum. *The menu never varied*. Sanitation in the kitchen and mess hall was unheard of. Everything was filthy.

After supper the warden entered the bullpen and called out the convicts who hadn't "kept the lick" that day. They were beaten with a leather strap six feet long, three inches wide and a quarter-inch thick — ten powerful lashes per man.

Finally the bull chain was drawn through the rings and the lights went out. Groaning with fatigue and despair Burns lay back on his cot and wondered if he were having a nightmare. Or was this the hell he had read of in Revelations? Or was he going insane?

Six days a week . . .

On Sunday the convicts were locked in the barracks and allowed to rest. By this time Burns' body and "stripes" were caked with filth, personal hygiene or cleanliness being out of the question during the week. The convicts had to sleep in their swamp-foul pants at night because it was a tremendous task to try to remove them through the ankle shackles.

On Sunday he was allowed a bath and given a clean pair of stripes.

That day he began to face the cold hard facts. The chain gangs were a vicious, medieval custom inherited from the slave trade of the 17th and 18th centuries. He knew he could not possibly endure such barbarous treatment for six to ten years. The brutal system would either kill him or drive him insane.

There were four old expressions on the chain gang and he started to give them some profound thought:

"Work out" — meaning serve your time.

"Pay out" — to purchase a pardon or parole.

"Die out" — to die or be killed in prison.

"Run out" — to escape! Also known as "To hang it on a limb."

To "work out" was impossible, and he knew it cost $2,000 to "pay out" or buy freedom. He had barely six dollars to his name.

So, he decided, *I'll die out trying to run out.*

The first step would be to get transferred to a smaller

camp, one where the gangs did not work on squad chains. The following Sunday he wrote a request for transfer to the prison commissioners, and two weeks later he and eleven other convicts were sent to a county chain gang in the backwoods.

There were no barracks here. Twelve men slept in a steel-barred cage on wheels called a pie wagon. There were four tiers of three bunks each and the convicts barely had room to turn around. Their bedding was lice-infested, half-decayed and sour-smelling. They washed in the open from a bucket. The mess hall was a foul shed inside the barbed wire stockade.

The convicts who failed to "keep the lick" were whipped in the yard — the victim being laid on a circular piece of corrugated iron. It was as bad as any other camp — but *they did not work on squad chains*, and that was all that mattered to Burns.

He knew he would be taking a desperate chance, because there were not only the chains and the guards and their guns to contend with, but bloodhounds as well. And if he failed in his attempt he would be thrown in the archaic horror called the sweatbox.

The box was three feet square and six feet high; too narrow for a man to lie down. It was exposed to the vicious sun, and the only ventilation was a few small holes bored near the top. Once a day the victim received a cup of water and a chunk of corn pone.

But he was willing to risk anything, even death, to escape the tortures and obsolete treatment of the chain gang. He decided to attempt his break on a Monday morning, while he was still somewhat fresh from his Sunday rest.

The big problem was the chains — how to get them off at just the right time. For six long weeks he worked on plan after plan, discarding most of them as idle and fantastic daydreams. Then —

The shackles around his ankles were circular, so if he could contrive to bend them into an elliptical shape he might be able to slip them over his heels. But how to bend them? They were made of steel as thick as a man's finger.

One day he noticed a huge Negro convict in his gang swinging a twelve-pound sledge hammer with such precision that he could hit the head of a pin with his eyes closed.

That was the answer. The Negro could hit his shackles and bend them into an elliptical shape. But Burns needed something solid to brace the shackles against, to take up the shock of the blow. A week later he found the second answer.

They were tearing up an old railroad. Burns fell in line to work next to the giant Negro. It was a day of terrific June heat and he waited until the guards were drowsy with the humidity. Then he whispered to the Negro.

"Sam, will you do me a favor? I've got six years to do for a crime I didn't want to commit. I'm going to try to hang it on a limb, and I need your help."

"Boss," Sam murmured, "if I can help you, I will."

"Well, Sam, if I put my leg against this railroad tie,

do you think you could hit my shackle hard enough to bend it?"

"Boss, I can hit it right plump."

He had to! If he missed, it might mean the loss of a foot. But life-or-death problems call for daring and courage. Burns, pretending he was crowbarring up a rail, placed his right foot against the tie. Sam was working right behind him. Burns glanced at the sleepy guards. Then he took a deep breath and closed his eyes.

"Shoot, Sam."

Sam swung the sledge and Burns winced as a shock of pain shot up his leg. Gritting his teeth he said, "Again!" And Sam swung another bull's-eye. Burns could barely get the words out. "Again, Sam." The sledge slammed the third time. Now the left foot. Sam delivered three carefully placed whacks with the sledge.

Sunset came and the convicts returned to camp and lined up before the pie wagons to have their chains checked. Burns' heart was riding in the back of his throat. Would the guard notice the elliptical shape of his shackles?

"Come by me . . . come by me . . ." It was Burns' turn. He stepped up and the squatting guard tugged at his chains. "Come by me . . ."

Safe! He crawled into his bunk and removed his shoes in the dark, greased his ankles and feet with spit and squeezed the shackles over his heel. It worked!

It was Wednesday night. Four days till Monday.

There were still the guards and their guns and the bloodhounds and miles of rough terrain to cross. Then he would have to get out of his telltale stripes and secure other clothes. Also, there was the fear that his Northern speech would give him away.

But none of it mattered. Come Monday, he was going — death, freedom or capture.

Monday, June 21 — the hottest day of the year. The gang was tearing up a small wooden bridge over a creek. Three convicts, one guard and Burns were on one side of the creek. The other convicts and guard and the three dogs were on the opposite side. Both banks were lined with catclaw thickets. It was 10 A.M.

Each convict was allowed two minutes for personal needs. Burns, nervous and taut, was ready for his turn. He called out.

"Getting out here!" This was his moment of truth. A chilly fear went up his spine as he waited for the guard's reply.

"All right, get out there." The guard pointed at the thicket.

Burns hobbled into the bushes, sat down, pulled off his shoes and started forcing his shackles over his heels. *Two minutes*, he thought frantically. *Two minutes.*

The first shackle was off. He struggled with the other one. Free! He put on his shoes and started crawling off through the underbrush. The two minutes were up.

"Come on, Burns. Get back to work!" the guard called.

If he didn't answer they would let loose the dogs. If he did answer the guard could tell from the direction of his voice that he was getting away. It was time to run. He sprang up and took off through the shrubbery in a fast crouching sprint.

"Man gone!" somebody cried, and a shotgun went *KA-WOW!*

Buckshot blazed through the brush. Burns picked up speed. The guard was yelling. "Burns is gone! Bring on the dogs!" *KA-WOW-WOW!* the second shotgun slammed both barrels, but Burns was going like the wind, and in a moment he was in the tupelo woods.

The trombone bay of the bloodhounds filled the hot air with dread music and within ten minutes of lung-bursting running the dogs were on him, howling, barking and snapping.

He had counted on this happening, and now he turned and faced them and tossed them little scraps of food he had saved up. He talked to them, called them by name, and actually got down on the ground to romp with them. It fooled the hounds completely. They thought he was playing with them.

He started running again, deeper into the woods, using the sun as his guide to the north. The joyful dogs kept right at his heels, having the time of their lives.

He ran — ran — through bushes, briars, hills, fields, woods, into a swamp. The sun was a white-hot branding iron and he was burning up. He plowed into a stream and sprawled in it, gulped water, and ran on. Within minutes he was scorching again.

But his feet and legs felt as light as air! For the first time in three months he was not lugging twenty pounds of chain.

Noon came and passed, and still he was racing along — legs aching, lungs gasping, his brain swimming with heat and fatigue, he kept at it. Had to. Life or death. Afternoon, 5 P.M., and he was still going strong, the yapping hounds still with him.

He broke into a clearing which contained a shanty. A Negro woman was bending over a washtub and a line of clothes was hanging over her head. Burns and his dog pack darted by the woman in a rush and he snatched up a pair of overalls and a shirt and kept right on going, the woman sending a startled howl after him. He dodged into a copse of pawpaws and changed clothes.

He reached a railroad trestle over a stream at six o'clock, ran to the middle of it and jumped into the cool water, and started drifting downstream. The unhappy dogs howled and whined and followed along the bank, but he lost them in half an hour. He crawled out of the water and took to the woods again.

At seven he stumbled out onto a paved highway and flagged the first northbound car. "How far are you going?" he asked.

"Just into the city."

"Well, if you have no objection, I'll go all the way with you."

"Sure. But it isn't far. Only about nine miles."

Nine miles! That meant he must have covered *twenty-seven miles* in his cross-country run.

Two police cars with shotguns sticking out of the sides tore by them going in the opposite direction.

"Wonder who they're after," the driver said.

"Moonshiners," Burns said promptly.

They were in the city before eight o'clock, and Burns got out in front of a used-clothing store. He bought a cheap pair of pants and a jacket for $2.50, which left him exactly $3.70. Then he entered a barber shop to get a shave.

The barber had no sooner laid him out in the chair and smeared his face with a soapy lather when a policeman came in and sat down to wait his turn.

"A New York gunman escaped from the chain gang this morning," he told the barber. "We've got a raft of posses out after him."

A nervous tremor ran through Burns and perspiration popped from his pores. All he could do was sit tight.

"What's he look like?" the barber asked.

"Short man about thirty," the policeman said. "We have orders to watch all railroads, bus stations and exits from the city."

The barber was finished with Burns and he swung up the chair. Fear was singing through Burns' body as he stood up and paid. His legs started to tremble as he walked to the coatrack to get his jacket. The policeman didn't even glance at him. Burns made for the door, pausing only when the barber called to him.

"Shave close enough?"

"Yes," Burns said. A close shave indeed!

He ate a cheap meal and selected a sleazy hotel that cost 75 cents for the night. He had to get off the streets and rest, and plan his next move. The desk clerk looked him over with an expression of startled wonder.

"So you hung it on the limb, huh?" he said.

Burns nearly dropped through the floor. Then he recognized the man. They had served time together when Burns first entered the chain gang. Talk about the long arm of coincidence!

The desk clerk, having no desire to see Burns recaptured, hurried him into a room for the night and offered him all the money he had. It was only six dollars and Burns accepted it gratefully. Then the clerk found some timetables and Burns set to work to figure out a route of escape.

The Nashville, Chattanooga and St. Louis Railroad, he found, had a train passing through the city station at 8:45 A.M., going to Chattanooga, Tennessee.

He couldn't sleep, because his mind was full of fearful problems. The police would be watching the station — how could he board the train without being spotted? He tossed and dozed fitfully. His friend woke him in the morning and gave him a pot of coffee and some hot biscuits. Then it was time to go.

He boarded a trolley, got off at the station, glanced at a clock and realized he had made a drastic miscalculation. It was only 8:15. He had thirty suspense-filled minutes to wait for the train. Surely some officer of the law would notice him in that length of time!

He steadied himself. He *had* to get through, and a cool head, calm nerves, quick thinking and quicker action should at least give him an even break. Putting on a bold front he walked into the station and purchased a ticket for Chattanooga.

He noticed that the train was chalked up on the bulletin board for five minutes late. *Another five minutes!* As he turned away he saw two typical sheriffs — shirt-sleeves, suspenders, pistols on hips — looking over everyone who entered the station.

His heart jumped violently. They were obviously looking for him, and he couldn't stay in the station. What should he do?

He had to act instantly — a hesitant manner would be suspicious. Summoning his courage he calmly walked toward the nearest exit. The two sheriffs moved to intercept him. Their eyes seemed to bore holes right through him as one of them spoke to him.

"Where's the next train going to, fella?"

Burns knew the sheriff knew where the train was going as well as he did. The question was a pretext, as the sheriff must have been in some doubt that Burns was the man he sought.

This was the supreme test. Nothing but courage could save him now. Facing the lawmen with a cool look he snapped out one word, "Chattanooga," and walked through the exit.

Thirty feet ahead was a drugstore. He walked toward it slowly, not looking back, entered and stepped up to the soda fountain and ordered a malted milk — with his eyes alternating between the clock and the entrance. The two sheriffs walked in behind him.

They went to the opposite end of the counter, facing him, and looked directly at him. Sweat broke over Burns and he strove desperately to control the trembling muscles of his face, which might register the fear in his brain. He had to get away from their direct iron-eyed gaze before he came unstitched.

Casually, he shifted around to the center of the counter. It placed him closer to them and gave them a profile view of him, but he was not compelled to look straight at them.

The clerk set the malted on the counter before him and Burns looked at it with dismay. He knew he couldn't pick it up to drink it without his hand trembling in naked fear. He could feel the tense, suspicious eyes of the sheriffs on him and he knew they were still debating in their minds whether or not he was their man.

He *had* to pick up the glass and drink.

His right side was away from the lawmen and he clenched his right fist with all his might, attempting to mesmerize himself and his muscles. Slowly he brought his fist up to the glass, relaxed it and picked up the glass. The trembling had stopped.

He drank the malt, picked up his check and went to the cashier, paid, and walked toward the door. The two sheriffs fell in behind him.

It's all up, he thought wildly. *When I reach the end of the cigar counter I'll make a break for it*. But his nerve faltered. He passed the cigar counter at a normal pace. He could hear the steps of the lawmen behind him.

I've got to run before it's too late! I'll do it when I reach the cosmetic counter. . . .

He went past the cosmetics. He couldn't get started, couldn't trust his trembling legs. The entrance was coming. *I'll take off at the door*, he promised himself. He strove desperately to control the screaming fear that was racking his body.

The door was ten feet away, the sheriffs ten feet behind him. He stepped through the doorway and turned left. *Now!*

He couldn't do it. His heart was a great lump riding sidesaddle in his chest. He thought he was going to pass out. *Just keep walking . . . get control of yourself. . . .*

He walked down the street to the station. It was the longest thirty feet he had ever walked. As he turned into the entrance, he noticed out of the corner of his eye that the two sheriffs were standing in front of the drugstore watching him go.

With the uncanny instinct of the hunted he knew in that moment that they had decided he was not the fugitive from the chain gang. He went on through the station unescorted.

It was 8:45. Still no train. He went out on the platform and stopped at a hotdog stand and ordered a Coke. He didn't want the thing but he had to occupy himself. A car pulled up at the end of the platform and a man in uniform got out.

"Who's that?" Burns asked the hotdog man.

"Chief of police."

"Does he always come down to see the train in?"

"No, never. He must be expecting someone, or looking for someone."

Trapped! It was all he could think of. The panic was on, and before he could scratch up a plan of action he saw three other men, plainclothed, walk over and speak to the Chief.

"Those are dicks!" the hotdog man said excitedly. "Something's up. Half the police force is down to meet the train."

The train's approaching whistle wailed. Burns was rooted to the spot. He couldn't think! He couldn't turn back now. The train was his only way out. He would have to take this last desperate gamble. But the law was standing there waiting for him!

The whistle blew for a grade crossing. It would be in the station in a few seconds. He set down the Coke bottle.

Start walking, he ordered himself.

The train was pulling in. Burns gathered his shaky strength and started walking toward it. Twenty-five feet to go . . . twenty . . . fifteen . . . a passenger door was standing open, waiting for him . . . ten feet . . . five . . .

"There he is! There he is! Get him!"

His heart missed a beat and electricity seemed to hum through his nervous system. He turned in helpless bewilderment. The Chief of police, the three detectives and a bunch of hangers-on were charging down the platform. Coming right for him!

He couldn't budge, couldn't think or act. His mouth dropped open and he thought he was going to scream. The urgent press of rushing men thundered down on him — and went right on by him without a glance!

He nearly fainted on the spot. Dazedly he turned and saw what had happened. A hobo was riding the rods on that train and someone had spotted him as it pulled in. The hobo, confused and frightened, had started to run. Now everyone was chasing him!

Burns had a clear path. He stepped aboard the train, entered a car and sat down. He was ready to collapse. Pandemonium was going on outside. The hobo had been caught and brought to the Chief. All the car windows were up, and Burns, crouching and trembling in his seat, could hear everything.

"This isn't the man we want!" the Chief cried. "We've caught the wrong man!"

Everybody was talking and milling around. The news started spreading through the train. A burly man standing right next to Burns' seat was telling another passenger all about it.

"A convict escaped from one of the camps yesterday! He's a vicious gunman from New York. Our police got a tip he would be on this train, but they mistook that hobo for him."

Sitting as still as a statue in the back of the car, Burns waited for the train to start with the numbness of despair. Wouldn't they *ever* get underway? The conductor felt the same way. He had a schedule to keep and the train was already late.

"All aboard!" he called, and gave the signal.

Clickety-clack, clickety-clack, the wheels were turning, the train was rolling thirty miles an hour. Burns started to breathe.

"Ticket, please," the conductor said.

Burns handed him his ticket. The conductor looked at it, looked at Burns and said, "Where did you get on?" Burns told him, but the conductor knew where he had gotten on as well as Burns did — only *he hadn't seen him get on*. He punched the ticket and walked away with a worried look. Which was just the way Burns felt!

The conductor held a whispered conversation with the brakeman. They both stole glances at Burns. He felt sick to his stomach. Would this nerve-racking suspense never let up? Now the conductor and his crew were suspicious of him, and they would probably wire ahead to the Chattanooga authorities. The law would be waiting for him in the station.

He picked up a timetable and went through it hurriedly, discovering that the train made a stop at a small town just outside Chattanooga. That would have to be his new station. But he would have to slip off the train without the knowledge of the conductor and crew.

He got up and took a seat near the door, and settled down to sweat out the long four hours to the little town. The train pulled into the station he wanted but he remained in his seat reading a paper, as if he had no intention of disembarking. The conductor gave him a searching look and turned away satisfied.

Just as the train started to leave Burns jumped up, stepped out of the car and hurried through the station. No one observed his departure.

One hour later he was walking down the highway to Chattanooga. And one week later he arrived in Chicago, a free man with sixty cents left in his pocket. Seven years later he was one of Chicago's leading citizens.

Within seven years Robert Burns became a successful Chicago publisher. Fantastic as it may be, *his own wife then turned him in to the law!* The chain gang demanded his extradition, but the state of Illinois refused to comply; they considered Burns to be an influential and valuable citizen. A great legal haggle followed and finally the chain gang offered a compromise: if Burns would voluntarily return to prison, they would give him a soft desk job and grant him a parole within three months. Against the advice of everyone, Burns agreed.

Returned to the South he was thrown back into the chain gang and told that he would have to serve his *full original sentence*. The entire country was outraged by this breach of promise, but the chain gang turned deaf ears to the demands for justice and fair play. Realizing that he had been tricked, Burns made another daring and successful escape in 1931. He was never recaptured, and for the rest of his life he lived as the famous Fugitive From A Chain Gang.

CHAPTER 10

The Whim of Chance

ON MAY 27, 1940, Wing-Commander Basil Embry's Blenheim was caught in anti-aircraft fire over Calais. When his motor failed he bailed out at 4,000 feet and landed in an orchard near St. Omer, which is at the extreme northern end of France. A patrol of German soldiers was waiting for him.

A small piece of flak had lodged in the fleshy part of his leg, but the wound seemed so minor that neither he nor his captors did anything about it. He was placed in a staff car and delivered to the German H.Q. where he was questioned about military information.

Divulging nothing but his name and rank, Embry was removed to a prisoner-of-war camp which was a large, overcrowded, wired enclosure, incredibly dirty. His leg was starting to trouble him a little by now, but not enough to worry him. He did not ask for medical attention.

An Irishman himself, he soon fell in with another Irish prisoner, Flight Lieutenant Treacy, who had been shot down over Calais a few days before Embry was captured. Treacy said the Germans intended to transport (by foot) all of their prisoners to a large camp

somewhere in the east, and the two Irishmen decided to attempt an escape en route.

Two days later the long column of prisoners was trudging along a French road.

The column was well guarded. No straggling was allowed. A truck with a mounted machine gun drove at the head of the column, and other armed trucks were placed at 150 yard intervals on down the line. The rear was watchdogged by troops with rifles and tommy guns. A motorcycle and sidecar (armed with machine gun) would drone past the prisoners from behind, park at the head of the column to watch it come by, and then rumble past them again.

Embry and Treacy counted the minutes between the time the motorcycle buzzed by them and they again overtook it. The time lag was in their favor. Another favorable point: they were tramping in the center of one of the 150-yard intervals between two armed trucks.

"Best to break when the column is on a long, straight stretch of road," Embry murmured to his friend. "That's the only time when the guards appear to relax their vigilance somewhat."

The apprehensive hours dragged by. Again and again Embry and Treacy keyed themselves up to the terrifying emotional peak of being right at the point of cutting and running — only to decide that the timing or the circumstances were wrong.

Every opportunity seemed to be only a half chance, never a whole one. The strain on their overwrought nerves was appalling.

The column took a turn and started down a long poplar-lined road. A signpost was standing on Embry's side of the road and he glanced at it — then looked again. It gave the name of the nearest village and, fantastic as it may seem, the name was *Embry!*

If ever a desperate man saw a good omen, this was it. The motorcycle had just hummed by. Embry took a quick glance around and, without a word or sign to Treacy, he plunged out of the column and between two poplars and dived into the ditch at the side of the road.

There was practically no cover in the ditch and he was in plain sight if anyone happened to look his way. But there had been no warning shout, so he knew no one had seen him break.

He lay still, playing possum. Dead men were a common sight along the roads of France in the spring of 1940.

When Embry dived into the ditch like a shot out of a gun, Treacy was left flabbergasted. Collecting himself, he decided that if one Irishman could make it so could another. Three hundred yards farther up the road Treacy leaped into the ditch. By then it was too late for him to try to cut back to find his friend; so Treacy took an entirely different route to freedom.

Embry, meanwhile, was in a bad position. Exposed to the German traffic along the road, his only hope was to cross an open field to a wood 300 yards off. A mighty risky task.

An old peasant woman was milking her cow in the field and she had seen Embry make his break. They looked at each other. Then she glanced at the road and made a signal: *Come on.* Embry started crawling into the field.

The old woman, still watching the Germans on the road, held up her hand: *Watch out.* Embry flattened in the dirt, waiting and watching for her next signal. In this manner, following the old woman's instructions, he managed to worm across the field and into the shelter of the wood.

He waved his thanks to the old woman and broke into a run.

The ten days that followed were nightmarish. The entire district was infested with German troops and the French peasants were too frightened to give Embry assistance as he stumbled south toward Paris.

Realizing he couldn't travel by daylight in his tattered RAF uniform he lifted an old coat and a pair of blue pants off a scarecrow, hoping to pass himself off as an itinerant Belgian.

He had little or no food. It rained constantly, and he had to sleep out in the wet weather. And now his wounded leg began to swell and pain. Finally, unable to hobble on, he had to operate on himself with a penknife — an agonizing ordeal which forced him to lay up for two days in a dripping wood to regain his strength.

It is in just such desperate straits that many escapers begin to lose their driving urge to seek freedom, and give themselves up; their resistance so reduced by hunger, exposure and pain that they become afraid to attempt to go on. The fear of death suddenly overshadows the desire for liberty. But Embry was gifted with an iron will that refused to bend. He went on.

He had to become an actor, passing on his very limited knowledge of the French language. German patrols would stop him and demand to see his identification, and he would start to flap his hands about in the Latin manner and tell his made-up story.

"My village was bombed out by your planes, monsieur. My papers were blown up with my wife and children. Now I am looking for my old mother who was last heard of in this district."

Time and again this somewhat feeble story got him by the German checkpoints. It is understandable. France had just fallen, the German occupational forces were only beginning to move in, and the entire countryside was a vast disorganization of homeless refugees wandering bewilderedly about — all of them telling tales similar to Embry's.

Passing through a village one day he bumped smack into three British tommies who, like himself, were trying to escape in stolen civilian clothes. Unfortunately, the three soldiers (unable to speak any French) had already attracted suspicion and a moment later were arrested by the Germans — along with Embry.

Protesting violently in his faulty French, he was taken to a German officer. He claimed he was a Belgian refugee. The officer turned out to be an interpreter who spoke perfect French!

Knowing his poor French would show him up, Embry thought fast.

"Monsieur," he said, "my native tongue is Flemish."

"Fine," the linguist officer said in Flemish. "I speak it."

But Embry did not — didn't know a single Flemish word! His situation was perilous. If the officer caught him in a lie, a very thorough and revealing interrogation would undoubtedly follow.

"Listen," Embry said in a low voice, "I must confess I have not been telling the truth. I am really a Gael."

"A Gael?" the officer wondered. "What's that? I've never heard of one. Where do they come from?"

"From Southern Ireland," Embry said on a wild and incorrect guess. The officer looked puzzled.

"Well — but what are you doing here in France?"

"I'm running away from the London police. I've

been in England blowing up pillar boxes and the police are on my track."

"Grand fellow!" The officer patted him on the back. "Good luck to your great work." Then, with a hint of suspicion, he said, "You speak Gaelic, of course?"

"Naturally," Embry said. "It's my native tongue."

"Well, say something in Gaelic then," the officer demanded.

Embry promptly rattled off the few words of Hindustani which he had picked up in India before the war.

"Good," the officer said. "That's Gaelic. I speak a little of it myself."

A minute later Embry was on the road to Paris again — still a free man!

As long as he was out of uniform (under international law he could be shot for this) and taking the risk of being captured as a spy in enemy-held territory, Embry decided to act the part and pick up what military information he came across to pass on to the British. He studied all German troop movements and convoys, noted the positions of their aerodromes and defenses, and put it all to memory.

One night, twenty days after his initial escape, he swam the Somme River and ran headlong into disaster — into a German patrol.

These men were of the new Gestapo breed and they were not the least bit gullible. They beat him up on sight, searched him, questioned him, and then hauled him to a German H.Q.

It was a large farmhouse in the shape of a U — the big courtyard closed off by a wall which contained the main gate. Embry was dragged across the yard past a huge manure pile which was overrun with ducks and pigs and chickens. He was conducted into the house and taken before a German captain.

As usual, Embry immediately launched into his Belgian refugee tale. This time, however, the story was not swallowed.

"I don't believe a word of what you say!" the German captain told him. "I think you are a British officer trying to escape. You are in civilian clothes and so, if you are what I think you are, you will be shot as a spy, tomorrow!"

Embry was finally thrown into a small storage room. An armed sentry stood at the door and another sentry took a post at the end of the corridor where it opened into the courtyard. Embry sat down on a box to contemplate his dire situation.

The interrogation had lasted all night and morning, and it was now past noon. Surely they would start in on him again that night — this time probably with an interpreter who spoke fluent French, and Embry would certainly be caught in his own lies.

To add to his anxiety he knew that the Germans had already posted notices in France warning that they intended to shoot all Allied combatants found out of uniform. There was no doubt in his mind that he was going to be shot as a spy the next morning.

So — his bluff was at an end. Now was the time for action.

He indicated to the sentry at the door that he was thirsty, and the German stepped down the hall to get him a drink. Embry was standing just inside the door when the sentry returned with a glass of water, and he hit the man with everything he had smack on the chin.

The German slammed back against the wall and dropped his rifle. Embry caught the falling weapon, reversed it and flattened the staggered sentry with one blow.

He stepped out of the door and started cautiously along the corridor, carrying the rifle ready at port arms. The second sentry was standing just outside the door in the courtyard, with his back to the exit. Embry leaped through the doorway at the same instant that the sentry wheeled about.

Embry caught him on the temple with the butt of the rifle and the German crumpled with a crushed skull. Taking in the courtyard at a glance, Embry saw it was deserted, and he raced along the side of the building toward the gate.

Just as he reached the passageway between the two wings of the building a German soldier came around the corner with a bucket of water in each hand.

The German stopped short, his mouth dropping open in astonishment, and let out a yell in the split second before Embry clubbed him down with the rifle butt.

A warning shout came from inside the building, and was answered by another from the sentry outside the closed gate. Caught in the open courtyard Embry looked around and saw the manure heap.

A haystack or any other sort of loose mound would have been far preferable — but escaping prisoners cannot be choosers. He plunged into the manure pile, scattering honking ducks, squawking hens and oinking pigs every which way, and frantically dug a hole for himself in the straw and muck.

Outraged Germans ran this way and that way, back and forth across the yard, in and out the gate and through the farm house — but not one of them stopped to think about the huge, foul mound in the center of the courtyard. Why should they? Surely nobody would be crazy enough to crawl into something like that!

Late that night a very evil-smelling escaped prisoner-of-war climbed out of the mound and slipped over the wall.

Later that week Embry came upon a bombed-out bicycle shop which was in a great clutter of bike parts. He stayed in the ruined shop for two days, constructing a complete bicycle out of odds and ends. Then he started pedaling toward Paris.

He had nearly reached the famed city when a German soldier stopped him and took the bike for himself. Embry finished his journey to Paris on foot. His leg had swollen again and he developed a painful limp.

Paris was already occupied by thousands of German troops, but many more thousands of French refugees were pouring in and out of the city every day and no one paid any attention to the dirty, tattered, limping Embry.

He went to the American Embassy and tried to pass himself off as an American tourist who had been caught in the backwash of war, and requested their assistance. The Embassy people recognized him immediately as

British and told him it was not in their power to help him. They did, however, give him 300 francs.

He spent a very bad time in Paris — prowling the streets by day and night, trying to find enough money to either bribe some official into helping him, or to purchase another bicycle. Once or twice he went so far as to step boldly up to prosperous-looking French civilians and tell them exactly who and what he was. They always gave him what money they could spare.

At one point he was picked up with some other homeless men and locked in a barred cage for nearly a week, living under ghastly conditions with the very dregs of the Paris underworld. Upon his release from jail, his luck took an upswing and he was finally able to lay his hands on a bicycle.

In one day he pedaled from Paris to Tours, a distance of 145 miles. With his painful leg now swollen to twice its normal size, this was truly a spectacular physical feat. Trying desperately to stay ahead of the advancing German armies which were now invading the South of France, he reached Limoges. To his despair he found that he could barely walk on his game leg.

He was admitted to the local hospital for treatment, but had to slip out within a few days and take to the roads again because the Germans were due to arrive in Limoges at any moment. Suffering greatly with pain, somewhat delirious from fever and possibly even gangrene, he made it to Toulouse and then to Marseilles.

Marseilles is on the tip of Southern France. Unaided, without food, money or shelter, tortured with pain, he had traveled by foot and bicycle from one end of the war-wracked, German-infested France to the other — a distance of over 500 miles as the crow flies.

His luck, which had depended from start to finish upon seizing the right opportunity on the spur of the moment and upon the whim of chance, held firm. He encountered two other escapees and all three of them were taken in by the French underground. Shortly thereafter they were smuggled out of France and into England.

I am happy to relate that a few months after their escape from the prisoner-of-war column, Embry and Treacy met once more in the RAF in England.

CHAPTER 11

The Fourth Man

LATE IN 1915, while the British forces were making their hopeless attack against the Turks at Gallipoli, Commander H. G. Stoker brought his submarine through the Dardanelles to enter the Sea of Marmara. The sub was immediately holed and sunk by a Turkish destroyer, and Stoker and his crew captured.

The Turks have never been known for their kindness toward prisoners of war, and they made no exception with Stoker. He was taken to Constantinople and thrown into a filthy, verminous cell where he was starved and ill-treated — the Turks unreasonably asserting that he was a reprisal for some imaginary injustice done to Turkish prisoners of war in Egypt.

They left him in the dark stinking hole for twenty-five days; alone, no one to talk to, nothing to do, feeding him a few foul scraps of food once a day. He was practically skin and bones when they finally dragged him out into the daylight and told him he was being transferred to Afion-Kara-Hissar, a prison camp in the middle of Turkey.

Afion-Kara-Hissar was in the vast open lands of

Anatolia and, for a prison camp, it was slovenly organized. Stoker saw at once that it would be comparatively easy to elude the sentries and break out of the place.

But Afion-Kara-Hissar was separated from the coast by 130 miles of wild, rugged, mountainous country — a wilderness where brigands and deserters roamed. And once the sea was gained, there were only a few places from which Greek islands could be reached.

Most of the prisoners Stoker talked to were of the opinion that it would be impossible for an escapee to cross this enemy country without food or water or outside assistance. The Turks seemed to be of the same opinion, because they kept a very loose surveillance over the camp.

Stoker, though he had no proof the task was possible, objected to having it deemed *im*possible until it had been tried; and, as yet, no one had ever actually attempted to escape from Afion-Kara-Hissar.

It was at this point that he met two other prisoners, an Englishman and a Scotsman. Both of these men were fed up with the starvation rations, bad treatment and their vermin-ridden quarters, and had separately been considering escape.

"I'm against the idea as long as the fighting continues on Gallipoli," the Englishman reasoned, "because any day now might bring about the fall of Constantinople, and then we would be released."

"All right," Stoker said grudgingly. "We'll wait and see what happens at Gallipoli."

More months of wormy bread and rancid meat, and lice, fleas, scorpions, hornets, wasps, mosquitoes and regiments of bedbugs, and the soul-numbing horror of endless and total inactivity. Then the Turkish commandant issued a startling bulletin: the British had given up their campaign and evacuated Gallipoli.

Stoker and his two friends would now have to effect their own release — and engage themselves in the old and deadly game whose stake was liberty.

They made their anxious preparations over a period of two weeks, saving up scraps of rations, making a rope and packs and even fashioning water bottles out of green canvas.

Their initial plan was simple. The window of the barracks in which they were imprisoned was set in an apparently sheer wall, and escape from it looked impossible because the drop to the ground was a breakneck height. But they had discovered two small ledges of molding under the window sill which would give them a foot-and-hand-hold and enable them to reach an adjoining roof.

On the appointed night, March 23, 1916, they took off their boots and hung them about their necks, coiled the linen rope around Stoker's waist, stuffed their packs with raisins and chocolate, and crouched under the window sill.

There were four sentries directly below them, lolling on a bench with cigarettes and conversation. Stoker climbed over the sill and felt for the lower strip of molding with his stocking feet. A moment later he was inching along like a fly on a wall, his two friends following him. None of the sentries looked up.

They gained the adjoining roof and found that the parapet was lower than they had expected. In order to take advantage of the sparse cover they had to lie flat on their stomachs and wiggle slowly toward the next roof.

It took them an hour to find a place where their rope would reach the ground. They tied one end to a convenient ring in the parapet and prepared to descend.

The guards' quarters were directly across the way from their position, and all at once a light went on in one of the upper rooms and a Turkish officer sat himself at the window to stare at the night. He was looking squarely at the three fugitives!

An anxious hour crawled by. Stoker and his two friends were afraid to move a muscle. Then the moon began to creep up the sky, preparing to flood the parapet with its silver radiance.

"We'll have to make a break for it," the Englishman whispered. "He'll see us in another minute!"

Stoker nodded and sucked his breath — and at that moment the Turk yawned and stretched and blew out his lamp. Stoker didn't hesitate. He slid over the edge and went down the rope, kicking a signboard over a doorway in his hurry. It clattered appallingly. The Englishman and Scotsman came down like shots.

In spite of the noise, no one came to investigate, and the three desperate men ran across the stockade yard, slipped through the barbed wire and raced into the moony dark. Freedom was 130 miles away — as the crow flies.

All escaping prisoners are in a highly strung, nervous

state and these three were under a severe physical strain as well, because a Turkish prison was not a health resort. Now they found themselves fleeing across a nightmare land, suspicious of every sound and shadow, and always with an unnerving *hunted* feeling behind them.

They had hoped to average fifteen miles a day if their food was to last. But after a ghastly night of toiling through the hills and great gray boulders they looked back in the dawn and saw Afion-Kara-Hissar only eight miles away. They thought they had covered *twice* that distance.

There wasn't a breath of air, or a jackal as far as the eye could see. Great fissures had cracked the floor of the valley they were in and the canyon walls sheared up as silent and bare as deserted ruins. The barren landscape made them think of dead ashes, and Stoker began to wonder if they had ended up on the other side of the moon.

There are some places on the globe where faith can waver, and this was one of them. Now that they had a chance to look around, they weren't sure they were still on the globe. It was like Death Valley doubled. Even the air was dead. Heat rained down through a silence as quiet as deafness, and the rocks lay around on shelves of pumice and granite like white bones.

They had no map of the country and had to steer by the stars. By daylight they were lost; by starlight they felt that they might have gone over the edge Columbus' sailors were afraid of — deep in a wilderness of canyons and barren mountains glowing in the cold moon like hills of scrap iron. Due south was their course, so they placed the polestar at their backs and tramped away from it — up and over and down anything that came in their way, which took them into some very strange, often weird, places.

Burning hills by day, intense cold at night; and sometimes, in the high places, several degrees of frost.

They knew within a few days out that they were making poor time, and they rationed themselves to two handfuls of raisins and two cups of cocoa a day. Hungry, thirsty, body-sore and utterly exhausted, and with the constant sense of being hunted, they trudged on.

A most unpleasant thing happened on the fifth day. Fearing that the water in his canvas canteen might be polluted, Stoker put a purifying pill in it. He was poisoned from the water within an hour. Possibly some adverse reaction was caused between the pill and the green coloring in the canvas.

The result was that he couldn't eat for two days and he became exceedingly lightheaded — to the point that he thought the Englishman and the Scotsman were two old friends of his who had been killed in 1914.

He couldn't seem to shake this obsession, even though he knew he was in the Anatolia wilderness, knew he was escaping from the Turks, and knew that he was engaged in a life or death business.

The Englishman and the Scotsman seemed to understand his delusion and they humored him as they plodded wearily on; and the odd part was that Stoker *knew* they were humoring him, yet he still remained mentally deranged on that one particular point, though perfectly sane and level-headed about everything else.

Gradually, as the effects of the poison wore off, his obsession began to fade and within four days it was gone. But it was to have a marked bearing on the inexplicable mystery that happened two nights later.

On the eleventh day of their escape the three hungry, dispirited and exhausted men approached the Taurus Mountains, which lay between them and the sea. There was a treacherous pass and they feared it would be guarded, yet they had to take it, as the mountains were impassable.

They started through the fissured foothills as sunset started slanting ochred shadows across the rocks and sending long gray shadows across the valley floor after them, like giant, reaching fingers.

They tramped in a line, separated by a dozen paces, thinking that if the leader bumped into anyone the other two might still have a chance to run for it. Stoker was in the end position.

Darkness swept down out of Asia and the valley was blotted by india ink. There wasn't a star in that blackness or a moon. A strong wind eddied and moaned through the crags causing an upper layer of sand to blow overhead, and the firmament was blanked out. A bad situation for men in a strange land without a compass.

The wildness of the night, the sense of impending danger, their total physical fatigue, all combined to react on their overstrained nerves. It was like a weird dream that bordered on nightmare — all so very unreal.

Their boots sent echoes up the canyon which died of

loneliness away up the towering cliffs against the sky. A kicked pebble would rattle across the rocks with the disturbance of a rat in a tomb, and every time they would pause to rest the silence flowed around them in a pressure that seemed to hurt their ears.

A few miles of walking by himself in the rear, in that solidified million-ton hush, and Stoker was suffering for companionship as avidly as thirst.

There was no water — only calcined cliffs and emptiness. They might have been the first men along that fissured pass since the time of Exodus. They felt insignificant among the skyscraper walls of stone.

A queer sensation crept over Stoker, something apart from his nervousness of fatigue or fright. A feeling of evil seemed to cloak this dismal landscape, a sort of repugnance mixed with fear, causing the sort of shudder a man might experience on brushing against a leper or standing before an empty house with the blinds drawn, on a mysterious street. There was something about that drafty emptiness of stone that was bad.

A sudden panic came over him. He wanted to run, to make a lot of noise and get out of there. And at that moment the Scotsman hissed at him.

"There's a light ahead, Stoker!"

The three fugitives drew together, crept around a slaggy boulder and sighted a distant watchfire in a gloomy setback among the cliffs. Turkish sentinels without a doubt.

"We'll have to slip by them," Stoker said. "There's no other way out."

They reconnoitered in the sooty dark and discovered

that the lax Turks hadn't manned an outpost or picket. Stealthily, they crawled past the lighted setback. The reddish glow of the watchfire bathed the cliffs and clinkerlike floor a rusty color that trembled and flickered with the flames.

Stoker and his two friends slipped on into the dark, darting from rock to rock, which were mounded like slag along the pass. The smell of the fire followed them in the night, sulphurous and smothering.

They started marching in line again, the Englishman in the lead, Stoker in the rear. A moon that looked moldy was now sneaking over the high-hung sky, shedding wan beams through the break in the lofty peaks, touching the crouching rocks with gelid radiance that looked as cold as witch-shine.

Again a queer sensation crept over Stoker — a sensation that was so positive it shortly became a conviction. Someone was walking behind him!

He *knew* without even turning to look that they were no longer three men struggling along in a line, *but four*. A fourth man was following them and he was just where he should be, a dozen paces behind Stoker at the end of the line.

He didn't know what he should do — run on ahead? call out to the others? or simply turn and confront the mysterious stranger? He did nothing. He kept on trudging, mechanically.

In dreams the most extraordinary and impossible things often happen and the dreamer always accepts them quite naturally. In just that dreamlike way Stoker now accustomed himself to the fourth man's presence.

Every time they stopped for a few minutes rest Stoker observed that the fourth man did not join them. He remained out of sight in the darkness; yet when they rose and resumed their march, he stepped into his place at the end of the line and followed them.

He never spoke, never changed his position; yet his presence seemed to give Stoker the courage and fortitude that one gets from a loyal friend when in a tight spot. It was as if he had said, "I cannot help, but when danger is at hand remember always that I am here, to stand or fall with you."

Stoker was convinced that he was suffering from a recurrence of his earlier obsession, that he had gone lightheaded again, and so he said nothing about the fourth man to his two friends. They had enough problems without thinking that he had gone out of his mind.

He tramped on with a great uplifting of spirit — hunger, thirst and exhaustion now forgotten; quite content to believe that the fourth man was there and was lending him strength and comfort throughout the most arduous part of the trying night.

Pressing on with greater determination and vigor than ever, the fugitives made their way through the mountain pass and down to the less dangerous plains just before daylight. With a sense of utmost relief Stoker turned and looked back.

The fourth man had vanished.

Striding forward with the dawn they got their first view of the sea. The beach far below was a ragged thread of lime, and not far from the shoreline a saffron fog was banked up under the sky to blot the horizons. Daylight spread over them and they sought shelter in a cave.

They made a fire and restored their strength with hot cocoa; but they were all strangely silent, as if afraid to speak. Stoker had no intention of telling his two friends about his weird hallucination, fearing that they would naturally believe he was having another delusion.

Finally the Scotsman, dourest of the three, spoke.

"This will no doubt sound crazy — but did either of you have the feeling last night that a fourth man was with us?"

Stoker was thunderstruck! Was it possible he hadn't had a hallucination? Had he *really seen the fourth man?* Then the Englishman cleared his throat.

"I hesitated to mention it," he said, "but the truth is — I *saw* the fourth man."

They both looked inquiringly at Stoker. He nodded dazedly, and said, "Yes, I saw him. He stayed with us all through the most difficult part of the night."

It is never surprising when an individual person imagines he sees things that don't exist, but how was it possible that *three separate individuals* could imagine the exact same thing?

Talking it over, they all agreed that the fourth man had joined them right after they slipped past the Turkish watchfire; they agreed that he had always walked at the end of the line, had remained out of sight every time they rested, and that he had never spoken; and they all agreed that his presence had given them a comforting sense of friendship and strength. And finally they were agreed that he had left them the moment they were out of danger.

What possible answer would explain this inexplicable mystery? The same identical hallucination, apparition or mental delusion had come to each of them at the same time and in the same way its presence had brought them great luck, giving them the strength and courage to cover the longest distance they had so far attempted in one trek, and got them past the mountain barrier which they had feared would mean their recapture.

Awed and bewildered they left the cave and started on the last leg of their strange passage to the sea.

Stoker's experience occurred in Asia Minor in April 1916. In May 1916, Sir Ernest Shackleton, the Antarctic explorer, and his party were marooned in the ice of South Georgia, some 8,000 miles away. Shackleton and two other men, Worsley and Crean, started to trek across the icy wasteland in a desperate attempt to reach help.

During the long arduous struggle across the unnamed mountains and treacherous glaciers it seemed to Shackleton *that a fourth man was with them.* Doubting his sanity he said nothing about it to his two companions. Then, when they had reached a point of safety, Worsley said to him:

"Boss, I had a curious feeling on the march that there was another person with us."

Crean then confessed that he too had felt the presence of a fourth man during the time when they were hard pressed.

Shackleton could offer no material explanation for the fourth man. His only comment was, "One feels the dearth of human word, the roughness of human speech in trying to describe things intangible."

Who was, or is, the Fourth Man? Is he perhaps the very spirit of Escape? Remember — *flight is a matter of luck, but freedom is the will of God.*

I am puzzled to relate that right after the time the Fourth Man left Stoker and his two friends, their luck turned against them. They were held up by brigands, robbed, threatened with death, and finally recaptured by the Turks.

Index

Afion-Kara-Hissar, 174, 175, 178
Alcatraz, 71
All Saints' Day, 99
American army, 55
Anatolia, 175, 179
Angel of Death, 91, 92
aqueduct, 41
Arnold, Benedict, 46
Asia, 180
Asia Minor, 185
Asquino, Count, 88, 92
auger, 33
Austria, 42
Avenue de St. Antoine, 41

Balbi, Friar, 88-90, 92-96, 98-102
Barracuda, 132
Bastille, 29, 30, 37, 42
bedbugs, 176
Belgium, 42
Bennington, 46
Berlin, 28
Bernardino, Private Pedro, 106-121
Bible, 90
Bishopsgate workhouse, 56
Blenheim, 162
Bonnot gang, 123
Braunau, 17

braziers, 45, 47, 50
Brazil, 134, 138, 140
Breton coast, 71
British Guiana, 124
Burgoyne, 46
Burns, Robert Elliot, 141-161
Byam, John, 43-48, 50-55

Calais, 162
Camopi River, 134, 135, 138, 140
Canada, 46, 55
candlestick, 32, 33
cannon, 38
Casanova de Seingalt, 87-103
"Castle, the", 58
Cayenne, 122-124
caymans, 138, 139
Champlain, Lake, 46
chapel, 62, 63, 96
Chattanooga, Tennessee, 154, 155, 160
Chicago, 160
chocolate, 176
Clinton, N.Y., 43
cocoa, 179
Committee of Safety, 43
Connecticut, 43
Constantinople, 174, 175
Continental army, 43

copper, 45
Crean, 186
Cyclops, 33

d'Aligre, 29-38, 40-42, 71
Danzig, 18
Dardanelles, 174
Day of the Dead, 99
Death or Freedom, 23
Demerara, 124
De Vargas, Captain Hernan, 104-121
Devil's Island (Ile du Diable), 122, 124, 125
Diable, Ile du (Devil's Island), 122, 124, 125
Dieudonné, 123-130, 132-140
Doges' Palace, 87, 94, 101
Dupont, 72, 74, 76, 77
Dutch Guiana, 123

Edgeworth Bess (Bess Lyon), 56-58
eels, electric, 136-139
Egypt, 174
Embry, 164
Embry, Wing-Commander Basil, 162-173
England, 168, 173
Euston Road, 68
Exodus, 181

Finchley, 58
fleas, 175
Fort Stanwix, 46
France, 140, 162, 165-167, 172, 173
Frederick the Great, 12, 13, 18, 103
French Guiana, 122-124, 128, 130, 134, 136, 140
French Revolution, 10, 28
Fugitive From A Chain Gang, 161
Fusina, 101, 102

Gallipoli, 174-176
Gelfhardt, 21-23
German H.Q., 162, 168
Giant's Staircase, 101
Giltspur Street, 66, 67
Giudecca, canal of the, 102
Glatz, fortress of, 12, 13, 17
Glatz, governor of, 13, 14, 17, 22
Grand Rounds, the, 35, 37, 38, 40
Gray's Inn Lane, 68
Guiana Indians, 134-138
guillotine, 10

handcuffs, 44, 58, 59
Health, Islands of (Iles du Salut), 122, 125, 130
Hessians, 46
highwayman, 56
Holland, 42
hornets, 175

India, 168
Inquisition, the, 87
iron hooks, 33

"Jacob", 33
Jaschinsky, Colonel, 12
Java, 123
jimmy, 61-63, 95
Judas holes, 33

Kermen, Alaine Sieur de, 71-84, 86, 103

INDEX

King's Bench Ward, 62

ladder, 33-38
La Tour du Trésor, 37
Latude, Henri Masères, de, 29-38, 40-42, 59, 71, 103
Leads, the, 87, 89, 98
leg irons, 58
lice, 175
Limoges, 172
linen, 34, 35
London, 56, 58, 65, 69, 167
Long Island, battle of, 46
Lorenzo, 88-90
Louis XI, King, 78
Louis XV, King, 29, 30
Lyon, Bess (Edgeworth Bess), 56-58

Magdeburg, 18, 27
manta ray, 133
Mapes, 47
Marmara, Sea of, 174
Marowana, 124
Marseilles, 172
Mestre, 102, 103
"monkey, the", 33, 34
Mont St. Michel, 71, 73-75, 80, 83, 84, 86
Morgan, Daniel, 46
mosquitoes, 175

Napoleon, 109, 110
Napoleon's Peninsular War, 104
Nashville, Chattanooga and St. Louis Railroad, 154
National Gallery, 70
Needle's Eye, 115
Neiss, River, 17
Newgate prison, 44

Newgate Prison (London), 57-59, 70
New York, 159
Nouveau Camp, 124

Old Bailey, 58, 59
onion soup, 127

Paleolithic ancestor, 9
palisade, 14, 16, 17
Paramaribo, 123
Paris, 28, 29, 36, 165, 168, 171, 172
penknife, 13, 32, 33
pickpocket, 56
"Polyphemus", 33
Pompadour, Madame de, 29, 30, 71, 72, 103
Pontorson, 75, 76, 83, 84
Porte St. Antoine, 35, 36, 40
Portugal, 104, 105
Princeton, battle of, 46
Prussian army, 12
"puppy dog, the", 33

raft, 47, 50-53
raisins, 176, 179
rats, 29
Red Room, 61, 62, 67
Revolutionary War, 43
Robespierre, Maximilien, 28
Robin Hood, 56
Roussenq, 127
Royale, 122

St. Giles police station, 57
St. Joseph, Ile, 122-124, 128
St. Laurent prison, 124
St. Leger, General, 46
St. Mark's church, 94, 98

St. Mark's Square, 93
St. Martin's-in-the-Fields, 70
St. Michael's day, 89
St. Omer, 162
St. Sepulchre, 66, 68
Salut, Iles du (Islands of Health), 122, 125, 130
Sam, 147, 148
Saratoga, 46
Savio alla Secrittura, 99
saw, 33, 34
Schaarschmidt, 9-11
Schell, Lieutenant, 14, 16, 17
scorpions, 175
Seine, River, 36
shackles, 44
Shackleton, Sir Ernest, 186
shark, 125, 132, 133
Sheppard, Jack, 56-70
shoemaker, 69
Silesia, 12, 17
Simsbury Mines, 43, 46, 55
Somme River, 168
Soradaci, 90-92
South Georgia, Antarctica, 186
Star Fort at Magdeburg, 18, 20, 23, 27
Stark, John, 46

Stepney, 56
Stoker, Commander H.G., 174-186
Stone Ward, 62

Taurus Mountains, 180
Tories, 43, 46
Tottenham Court, 68
Toulouse, 172
Tours, 172
Treacy, Flight Lieutenant, 162-165, 173
Trenck, Baron Friedrich von der, 12-14, 16-28, 59, 87, 103
Trenton, battle of, 46
"Tubalcain", 33
Turkey, 174
Turks, 174, 175, 179, 181, 182, 186

Venice, 87, 88, 93
Vincennes, 29

Washington, 46
wasps, 175
watchman, 68
Wild, Jonathan, 57, 58
Worsley, 186

The Author

ROBERT EDMOND ALTER has written a dozen books for young people. When he left home at the age of sixteen, Bob Alter was determined to make social work his career. At twenty, after working as a citrus picker and at a score of other jobs, he found himself in the army. By the time he had reached his early thirties, he was back to an ambition he held even before his fascination with social work — he would be a writer.

Before his untimely death at the age of 40, he completed his many books for young people and his adult fiction was published in national magazines, including the *Saturday Evening Post* and *Argosy*.

www.ingramcontent.com/pod-product-compliance
Lightning Source LLC
LaVergne TN
LVHW041619070426
835507LV00008B/339